material obsession 2

More modern quilts with traditional roots

material obsession 2

More modern quilts with traditional roots

KATHY DOUGHTY and SARAH FIELKE

PHOTOGRAPHY BY

JOHN DOUGHTY

STC Craft · A Melanie Falick Book · New York

Contents

THE NOTION OF TWO   8

PROJECTS

Brighton Rock   12

Heaven & Earth   20

The Seasons   28

Kismet   38

Calling It Curtains   44

Playground Days   54

Jungle Boogie   60

Now & Then   68

Charlotte Sometimes   74

Over the Border   84

Sunday   92

Stashbuster   102

Coming Up Roses   108

Pop Stars   118

Maple Leaf Rag   124

Gypsy Kisses   132

Fruit Tingles   140

Bluebirds & Happiness   150

Looking Back   158

Jazz Hands   168

Erica's Honesty   176

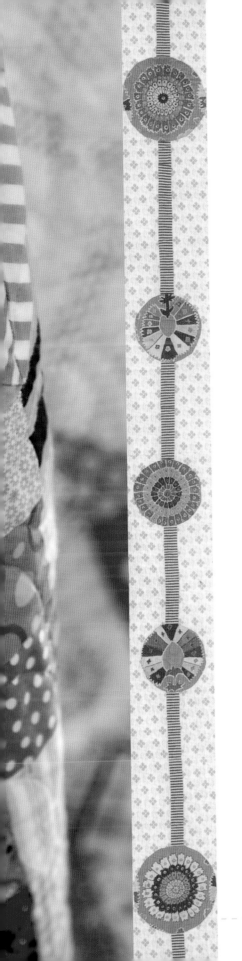

QUILTING BASICS — 184

Fabric for quilts — 186
Choosing threads — 187
Working with color — 188
Rulers — 190
Cutting shapes by hand — 194
Fussy-cutting — 195
Foundation-piecing — 196
Appliqué — 198
Quilt layout — 202
Quilt assembly — 204
Quilting — 206
Binding — 210

GLOSSARY — 214

INDEX — 216

ABOUT THE AUTHORS — 220

ACKNOWLEDGMENTS — 222

DEGREE OF DIFFICULTY

 Straightforward piecing

 May contain inset seams, intermediate piecing, or hand-appliqué

 Contains advanced piecing or appliqué techniques

 Complex piecing and/or a combination of more complex techniques

The Notion of Two

Making quilts connects quilters to each other. There is an innate process of sharing techniques, fabrics, and ideas that creates the quilting bee environment, something of give and take, while adding one's own personal style to an age-old craft. There is often a sense of connection to the archetypal quilting sisters who came before us, as well as to the one who sits next to us in our group, class, or life.

This book is about that process. We are fortunate to have contact with lots of passionate quilters. Our conversations through the day are often about fabric choices for blocks, borders, or backings ... as well as our families and lives. Maybe most people aren't as obsessed as we are ... or are they?

One of the things we have noticed as part of our quilting journey is how much inspiration is shared. We each often embark on a project at home and get very excited about the originality of the idea. One of us runs into the shop to show the other her work and finds the other one doing something similar! We have found ourselves, at times, working in the same direction by using either the same fabric or pattern, without being consciously aware of the other's actions. We pore over books or concepts and have to control the overwhelming desire to make it first. Instead of having this strong force hold us back, we decided to use it for this book. Our interpretation of each idea often starts in the same spot but ends up somewhere completely different.

As a result, the book is set out in ten pairs of quilts, each one springing from the same concept, be it one-block wonders, scrap quilts, or foundation-piecing. We have also included one quilt that we designed and made together.

Like most quilters, we are keenly aware of the perpetual search for inspiration. Some of us have it in excess and some struggle to identify just

what we are looking for, but either way, it comes in time. It can be elusive or brewing in the background, causing us to think, consider, and wonder, until the idea comes to life. In other cases, it is obvious and dramatic enough to cause us to jump into immediate action to satisfy the strong creative urge. Our ideas most often come from antique quilts; however, just as they did for those original quilters, ideas can sometimes come simply from looking out the window. We love the traditional, but done our way, using fresh new fabrics to bring old favorites to life in a new way.

The other important point about this book is that we, as quilters, have grown considerably over the past five years in the shop. We have moved on from the simple square, in all its magnificent glory, to other shapes and processes. As a result, this book presents more techniques that we have enjoyed experimenting with, and now we urge you to do the same! There are quilts that are slow-brewing as well as those that spring from an impulsive need to make a quilt NOW. There may be quilts that you want to make as you see them, or bits and pieces of these quilts that inspire you to interpret them in your own way. We hope you find new techniques to learn and experiment with for yourself, just as we did.

Perhaps you have always wanted to make a Lone Star, do foundation piecing, a scrap quilt, a medallion quilt, or maybe you have a piece of vintage fabric in your stash. If you think a block or quilt is "out of your comfort zone" . . . start with just one block and play with it. We hope the result will be that you take that idea and run with it.

Kathy and Sarah

Shared Inspiration

❧❧❧❧❧❧❧

There is only one quilt in this set, but the pair is us—we made it together!

It is a project to demonstrate working with color and using a 60-degree triangle.

It is a fun quilt to put together while exercising color balance and ruler techniques.

We started with the three different center fabrics in the blocks and built three piles of fabrics

from each colorway, adjusting and replacing until we had a color grade that pleased us both.

If you make this quilt, it is a good idea to take everything in your stash in the colors you are

using and separate them into piles to grade. Look at them through a camera, or squint your

eyes as you go, to see the different tones in the colors.

Brighton Rock

Brighton Rock

 Kathy Doughty & Sarah Fielke

THE IDEA

Using color is fun! Repeat after us: Using color is fun! What better place is there to start than with a pile of Kaffe Fassett fabrics and one of our favorite tools, the 60-degree ruler? And if you really want to experiment, a color wheel can be handy too. We chose a primary triad of red, blue, and yellow.

Select lots of color variations in each group—moving from light to dark, or into its neighbor's space on the color wheel—without reading your fabric choices too literally. This is a great quilt to make from your stash in our colors or in a group of your own favorites.

Finished quilt size

Throw, 52½ x 58½ inches
Finished block size: 14 inches from side to side; 16 inches from point to point

Materials and tools

⅝ yard each of three swirl print fabrics for hexagon centers and border
¼ yard each of six red-print fabrics
¼ yard each of six blue-print fabrics
¼ yard each of six yellow-print fabrics
1 yard background fabric for setting triangles
⅞ yard brown fabric for Inner Border and binding
3⅛ yards backing fabric
59 x 63 inches cotton batting
Neutral-colored cotton thread for piecing
Rotary cutter, quilter's ruler, and cutting mat
Creative Grids 60-degree ruler
Brown perle cotton no. 8 for quilting

NOTE: *It is recommended that all fabrics be 100 percent cotton, and be ironed. Requirements are based on fabric 44 inches wide. Unless otherwise stated, all seam allowances are ¼ inch throughout. Color test any dark fabrics that you are using (see page 189), and wash them before cutting if they run.*
  Please read all instructions before starting.

Diagram 1

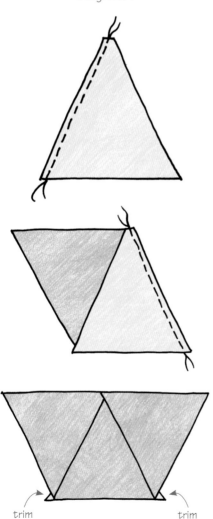

Cutting

All fabrics are strip cut across the width of the fabric from fold to selvage unless otherwise specified, or unless you are using a directional print (cut off all selvages first). It is advisable, when starting a new project, to make one complete block first, to ensure all the measurements are right before cutting all the fabric.

FROM EACH OF THE THREE SWIRL-PRINT FABRICS, CUT:
- Four strips, 3½ inches wide. Cross cut into 60-degree triangles, using the 60-degree ruler (see Rulers on page 190). You will need eighteen 60-degree triangles from each fabric for the hexagon centers (54 triangles in all), and 106 triangles and eight half-triangles for the Outer Border.
- Four 3½-inch squares, for the Outer Border corners.

FROM EACH OF SIX RED-PRINT FABRICS, CUT:
- Three strips, 1½ inches wide.

FROM EACH OF SIX BLUE-PRINT FABRICS, CUT:
- Three strips, 1½ inches wide.

FROM EACH OF SIX YELLOW-PRINT FABRICS, CUT:
- Three strips, 1½ inches wide.

FROM BACKGROUND FABRIC, CUT:
- Four strips, 7½ inches wide. Using the 60-degree ruler as before, from two of the strips, cross cut twelve 60-degree triangles. Fold the remaining strips in half, wrong sides together, and, using the ruler as before, cross cut 12 half-triangles, two at a time, in order to get six right-facing and six left-facing half-triangles.

FROM BORDER FABRIC, CUT:
- Five strips, 2½ inches wide, for the Inner Border.
- Six strips, 2½ inches wide, for the binding. Sew the strips together, end to end, using 45-degree seams, and press seams to one side.

Constructing the quilt top

HEXAGON BLOCKS (MAKE 9)

1 Take the 18 triangles cut from each of the three swirl fabrics and divide each color into three sets, each with six triangles.
2 To make each of the nine blocks, take one set of six triangles and, with right sides together, match the blunt points of two triangles (Diagram 1). Stitch one of the angled sides of the triangles together.

Make two pairs and then join a third triangle to each pair, matching the blunt points and pinning through the join to obtain a neat point.

3   There are now two sets of three triangles. Pin them carefully together along the straight edge and join. Snip off all the extending "ears" to reduce bulk.

4   Make the center hexagons for all nine blocks in the same manner. When you have completed nine hexagons, it is time to add the strips.

5   Rehearse the color for the strips around the hexagon centers on the design wall (see page 202). Place one hexagon center on the wall and arrange strips around it, working loosely from light in the center of the block to dark at the outside. The manner in which you arrange the strips will determine how scrappy or organized your quilt will look. For an organized look, choose strips that very obviously go from light to dark. For a scrappy look, switch the fabrics around, with less attention to grading the value of the strip.

6   Position the first strip so there is a 2-inch overhang at the start of the seam. Start sewing ½ inch in from the edge. (The extra fabric and the partial seam are required to finish the first round of the hexagon.) Place a pin at the beginning of this strip to mark it as the starting point. Fold the strip back and finger-press open.

TIP: *Take care not to press the block out of shape as the rounds are added to the hexagon. Place the iron on top of the fabric but do not push in any direction.*

7   Using the 60-degree ruler and rotary cutter, trim the edge of the strip flush with the next side of the hexagon (Diagram 2). Accurate cutting of the strips and precise ¼-inch seams are very important to maintain the hexagonal shape.

8   Move to the next side of the hexagon, pin the strip of fabric in place, and stitch. Fold the strip back and finger-press open. Using the ruler and rotary cutter, as before, trim the edge of the strip flush with the next side of the hexagon.

9   Continue in this manner until the last side of the hexagon is reached. Fold the excess strip back so the right sides of the strips are together and stitch. Trim all seams and press flat.

10 Add another three rounds of strips in the same manner.

ASSEMBLING THE BLOCKS

11 Using the photograph of the quilt as a guide, arrange the blocks into three rows of three hexagonal blocks. Distribute the fabrics and colors evenly across the surface of the quilt. It is a good idea, at this point, to use your design wall, so you can rearrange the blocks until you are happy with the color placement.

Diagram 2

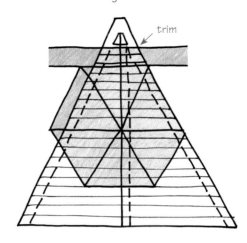

Quilt Assembly Diagram

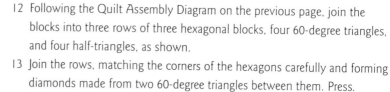

12 Following the Quilt Assembly Diagram on the previous page, join the blocks into three rows of three hexagonal blocks, four 60-degree triangles, and four half-triangles, as shown.

13 Join the rows, matching the corners of the hexagons carefully and forming diamonds made from two 60-degree triangles between them. Press.

INNER BORDER (BROWN)

14 Measure the width of the quilt through the center in both directions. It should measure 42½ x 48½ inches. (If your measurements differ, you will need to adjust your border measurements.) Trim two of the brown Inner Border strips to 2½ x 42½ inches. Join the remaining three strips of brown fabric together, end to end, to create one long strip, and cut two strips, each 2½ x 52½ inches.

15 Find the middle of one of the shorter strips and the middle of the top edge of the quilt top and pin. Next, match and pin the ends, and then pin the edges in between. Sew the shorter strips to the top and bottom of the quilt top in this manner. Press.

16 Stitch the longer strips to each side of the quilt top in the same way. Press.

OUTER BORDER (TRIANGLES)

17 Join 60-degree triangles cut from the swirl fabrics to make two strips of 25 triangles and two strips of 28 triangles. It is helpful to develop a pattern to keep the colors balanced.

18 Sew a half-triangle to the ends of each strip to make them square.

19 Find the middle of one of the 28-triangle strips and the middle of one long edge of the quilt top and pin together. Next, match and pin the ends, then pin the edges in between. Sew both 28-triangle strips to the sides of the quilt top in this manner and press the seam allowances toward the Inner Border.

20 Stitch a 3½-inch square to each end of the remaining two borders and press the seam allowances toward the squares. Join the strips to the quilt top, as before, and press. Your quilt top is complete!

Backing, quilting, and binding

Cut the backing fabric crosswise in half, giving two 56-inch pieces. Remove the selvages and stitch the pieces together up the middle seam. Press the seam allowance open and press the backing piece carefully.

Refer to pages 204–211 for instructions on finishing.

Brighton Rock is hand-quilted using brown perle cotton no. 8. The triangles are outline-quilted at the center of the hexagonal blocks and in the ditch at the joins of the strips. The background triangles are quilted with lines of stitching echoing the shape of the diamonds, and alternate triangles in the Outer Border are outline-quilted ⅛ inch from the edge.

Shared Inspiration

~:~:~:~:~:~:

We were lucky enough to spend some time with Kaffe Fassett and Brandon
Mably while hosting their quilting workshops. At the end of a fun-filled and
creative week, Kaffe gave each of us equal amounts of his lavender Minton
fabric and challenged us to use it. As you can see, the final outcome is
very different, but each quilt sprang from the same place.

The Seasons

Heaven & Earth

Heaven & Earth

 Kathy Doughty

THE IDEA

When I look at this quilt, I go back in time to my after-school walks in the woods behind my house. The stars are the heavens and the border is the soft forest floor. Technically, Heaven & Earth is a tri-color quilt of purple, orange, and green. When making a "color exercise" quilt, I start out gathering strictly defined color options, and then push the limitations on the color wheel. The variety of contrast and values keeps the eyes bouncing from star to star throughout the quilt, until they settle on the warm earthy colors of the border. My quilt group gasped at the border choice. However, I see it as my mission to push boundaries, or borders, as the case may be. These choices relate to my inner voice; let yours make your choices for you!

Finished quilt size

Queen, 79½ x 102½ inches

Block size: 12 inches, including seam allowance

Materials and tools

4¼ yards dark purple background fabric

⅛ yard of 24 different fabrics for the stars (or proportionately more if using fewer fabrics)

2¼ yards light purple background fabric

1½ yards border fabric

¾ yard binding fabric

6¼ yards backing fabric

87 x 110 inches cotton batting

Rotary cutter, quilter's ruler, and cutting mat

Neutral-colored cotton thread for piecing

NOTE: *It is recommended that all fabrics be 100 percent cotton, and be ironed. Requirements are based on fabric 44 inches wide. Unless otherwise stated, all seam allowances are ¼ inch throughout. Color test any dark fabrics that you are using (see page 189), and wash them before cutting if they run.*

Please read all instructions before starting.

Block 1

Diagram 1

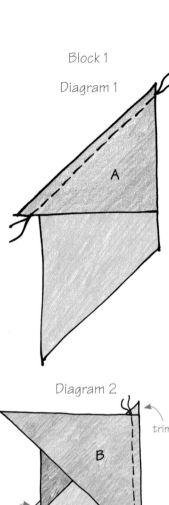

A

Template

If you are not using the 45-degree line on your quilter's ruler, trace the Template 1 diamond (on the pattern sheet) onto template plastic with a sharp 2B pencil. Cut out accurately with sharp scissors—not fabric scissors!

Cutting

All fabrics are strip cut across the width of the fabric from fold to selvage unless otherwise specified (cut off all selvages first).

FROM EACH OF THE 24 STAR FABRICS, CUT:

- One strip, 3 inches wide. Using Template 1 or your quilter's ruler on the 45-degree angle, cross cut each strip into eight diamonds with a 4¼-inch side, until you have 192 diamonds in a variety of colors. Set them aside in 24 sets of eight, for the stars in Block 1.

FROM DARK PURPLE BACKGROUND FABRIC, CUT:

- Eight strips, 3⅜ inches wide. Cross cut into 96 squares, each 3⅜ inches. Cross cut these squares on the diagonal, giving 192 half-square A triangles (eight per Block 1).
- 11 strips, 4⅜ inches wide. Cross cut into 96 squares, each 4⅜ inches. Cross cut these on the diagonal to make 192 half-square B triangles (eight per Block 1).
- Three strips, 4½ inches wide. Cross cut into 24 squares, each 4½ inches, for the centers of Block 2.
- 24 strips, 2¼ inches wide. Cross cut into 96 rectangles, each 2¼ x 9¼ inches, for Block 2.

FROM LIGHT PURPLE BACKGROUND FABRIC, CUT:

- 18 strips, 2¾ inches wide. Cross cut twelve of these strips into 48

Diagram 2

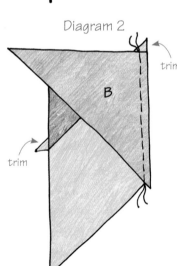

B

trim

trim

Diagram 4

Diagram 3

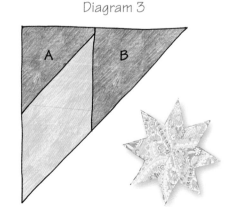

A   B

A

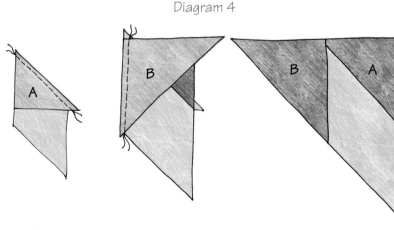

B

B   A

rectangles, each 2¾ x 9 inches. Cross cut the remaining six strips into 48 rectangles, each 2¾ x 4½ inches, for Block 2.

- Six strips, 4⅜ inches wide. Cross cut into 48 squares, and then cross cut the squares on the diagonal to make 96 half-square triangles for the corners of Block 2.

FROM BORDER FABRIC, CUT:

- Nine strips, 5½ inches wide. Sew them end to end and set aside for borders.

FROM BINDING FABRIC, CUT:

- Nine strips, 2½ inches wide. Join the strips, end to end, using 45-degree seams, and press seams to one side.

Constructing the quilt top

BLOCK 1 (MAKE 24)

1 Lay out the star point diamonds. Sew an A triangle to one side of a diamond (Diagram 1). Trim the ears and pin all points as you go.

2 Pin and sew the straight edge of a B triangle to this unit (Diagram 2). Press open (Diagram 3). Make four of these units.

3 Following Steps 1 and 2, make another four units, creating the mirror-image of the first four (Diagram 4).

4 Keeping the star pattern correct, sew the units together into pairs, along the diagonal edge, creating four squares (Diagram 5), and then join the squares into pairs (Diagram 6). Now join the pairs to complete Block 1 (Diagram 7). Trim the block to 12 inches square, if necessary. Make 24 blocks in this way.

Diagram 5

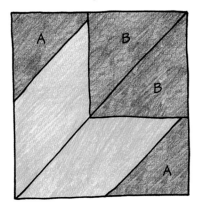

Diagram 6

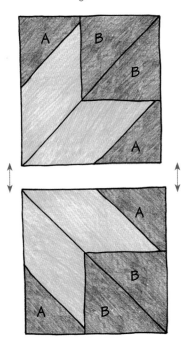

Diagram 7
Finished Block 1 (includes seam allowance)

Block 2
Diagram 8

Diagram 9

BLOCK 2 (MAKE 24)

5 Sew 2¾ x 4½-inch light background rectangles to opposite sides of a 4½-inch dark background center square (Diagram 8). Press the seams toward the dark center.

6 Sew 2¾ x 9-inch light background rectangles to both sides of the unit created in Step 5 (Diagram 9). Press the seams toward the dark center.

7 Match the middle of one dark 2¼ x 9¼-inch strip to the middle of one side of the unit created in Step 6. There will be ⅛ inch over on both ends. Sew and press the seam allowance toward the dark strip. Repeat this process on all four sides (Diagram 10). Do not trim the excess.

8 Finger-press this new unit in half and finger-press a light-colored 4⅜-inch corner triangle in the same manner. Match the pressed center points and sew together (Diagram 11). Use your ruler to trim excess border fabric even with seam allowance of the triangle (Diagram 12). Repeat for each corner, completing Block 2 (Diagram 13). Trim the block to 12 inches square, if necessary. Make 24 blocks in this way.

ASSEMBLING THE BLOCKS

9   Assemble the blocks in eight rows of six, alternating Blocks 1 and 2, and laying them out first for color balancing. Number each row from top to bottom and sew the first block to the second block for all rows. Leave all connecting threads uncut until you are finished with all eight rows. Then start sewing Block 2 to Block 3 for all rows. Do this until the quilt rows are assembled.

10 Now sew the first row to the second, the second to the third, and so on until finished. Press.

Diagram 10

Diagram 11

Diagram 12

Diagram 13
Finished Block 2
(includes seam allowance)

11 Measure the quilt top through the center in both directions. It should measure 69½ x 92½ inches. (If your measurements differ, you will need to adjust your border measurements.) From the joined border strip, cut two strips, each 5½ x 92½ inches, for the side borders, and two strips, each 5½ x 79½ inches, for the top and bottom.

12 Find the middle point on the side edge of the quilt top and the middle of one of the side border strips. Pin the middles together, match the ends, and pin, and then pin securely the length of the quilt to ensure the two pieces are equal. Sew the side borders in place.

13 Repeat for the top and bottom borders. Your quilt top is complete!

Backing, quilting, and binding

Cut the backing fabric crosswise in half into two 112-inch pieces. Remove the selvages and stitch the pieces together up the middle seam. Press the seam allowance open and press the backing piece carefully.

Refer to pages 204–211 for instructions on finishing.

Heaven & Earth is a flood of color and pattern. When I make a quilt like this, I often machine-quilt it due to the fact that hours of hand-quilting, although beautiful, will not really make an impact. The power of the quilt is in the saturation of the fabrics used. So I selected a loose quilting pattern with flowing lines throughout. I suggest that machine-quilting patterns be enlarged to 6- or 8-inch repeats to allow the quilt to stay soft and comfortable.

HEAVEN & EARTH 27

The Seasons

 Sarah Fielke

THE IDEA

I was having trouble with this project at first. My natural preference is bright, happy, clear colors, and I found the lavender fabric quite cold and hard to match. Thinking about the word "cold" in relation to color, I saw the gray fabric, and the two together seemed to sing out "Winter."

From there, the color choices were easy. Bright, lush greens for summer, rich reds and deep oranges for fall, and pretty pastels for spring. Amazing! All these colors seemed to work with the lavender once I had come to the concept.

This quilt also uses one of my favorite tools, the 18-degree wedge ruler. I highly recommend investing in this ruler . . . I do caution you, however: it has a high addiction warning!

Finished quilt size

Wall-hanging, 53¼ x 54¼ inches
Block size: 21½ x 22 inches, including seam allowance

Materials and tools

⅝ yard multicolor-spotted fabric for Summer block background
⅝ yard gray fabric for Winter block background
⅝ yard orange-toned fabric for Fall block background
⅝ yard pink-spotted fabric for Spring block background
6 inches each of three contrasting fabrics for the "ground"
⅝ yard each of four brown fabrics for trees and Inner Border
1¼ yards purple feature fabric
⅛ yard each of different fabrics to represent the leaves of each season: 9 green for Summer, 7 reds and oranges for Fall, and 10 pinks and light greens for Spring (scraps will be used for appliqué)
½ yard brown-and-green-spotted fabric for binding
3½ yards backing fabric
63-inch-square cotton batting
Blue beads and rickrack for Summer flowers (optional)
Clear crystal beads for ice in Winter (optional)
Template plastic, silver gel pen, and appliqué glue
Appliqué needles and cotton thread to match appliqué fabrics
18-degree wedge ruler (optional)
Rotary cutter, quilter's ruler, and cutting mat
Neutral-colored cotton thread for piecing
Perle cotton no. 8 in dark brown, white, variegated brown/red, and variegated pink/green for quilting

NOTE: *It is recommended that all fabrics be 100 percent cotton, and be ironed. Requirements are based on fabric 44 inches wide. Unless otherwise stated, all seam allowances are ¼ inch throughout. Color test any dark fabrics that you are using (see page 189), and wash them before cutting if they run.*

Please read all instructions before starting.

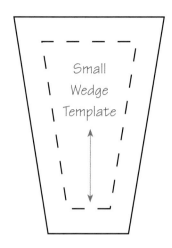

Small Wedge Template

Templates

Trace all the appliqué shapes (both on these pages and the Large Tree on the pattern sheet) onto template plastic using a sharp 2B pencil. If you are not using an 18-degree ruler, trace the Small Wedge (left) and Large Wedge (on the pattern sheet). Cut out all shapes accurately using sharp scissors—not fabric scissors! Label your templates.

Cutting

All fabrics are strip cut across the width of the fabric from fold to selvage unless otherwise specified (cut off all selvages first).

NOTE: *When cutting, remember to save all your scraps for the small appliqué shapes.*

FROM EACH OF THE BLOCK BACKGROUNDS, CUT:

• One rectangle, 21½ x 18 inches.

FROM THE THREE "GROUND" FABRICS, CUT:

• One rectangle, 4½ x 21½ inches.

FROM THE PURPLE FEATURE FABRIC, CUT:

• One rectangle, 4½ x 21½ inches, for the Winter "ground."
• Four strips, 1½ inches wide, for the Summer and Fall leaves.
• Six strips, 2¼ inches wide. Using the 18-degree ruler or the Small Wedge template, cut strips into 192 wedge shapes, for Inner Border.
• Five strips, 3½ inches wide, for the Outer Border.

FROM EACH OF FOUR DIFFERENT BROWN FABRICS, CUT:

• Two strips, 2¼ inches wide. Using the 18-degree ruler or the Small Wedge template, cut the strips into 198 wedge shapes, for the Inner Border.
• One square, 3½ inches, for the Outer Border corners.

FROM EACH OF THE LEAF FABRICS, CUT:

• One strip, 1½ inches wide.

FROM BINDING FABRIC, CUT:

• Seven strips, 2½ inches wide. Join the strips, end to end, using 45-degree seams, and press seams to one side.

Constructing the quilt top

STRIPPED LEAF CANOPIES

1 Separate each set of leaf fabrics into groups of 10 strips. The Summer set will include one strip of the purple feature fabric and the Fall set includes three.

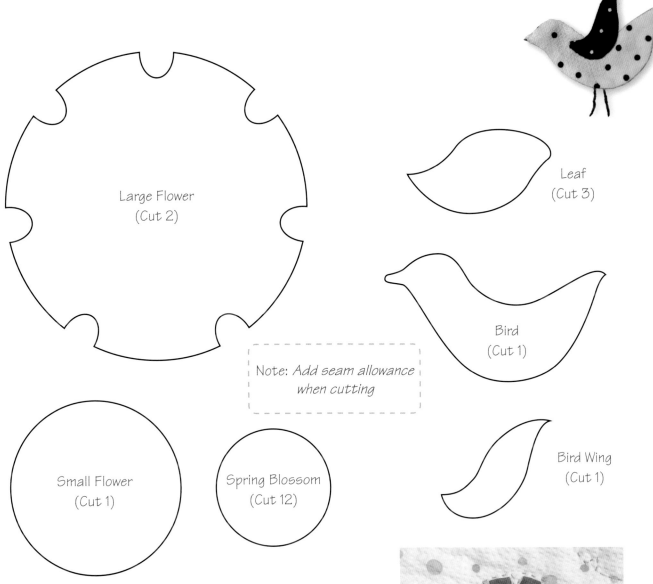

Large Flower
(Cut 2)

Leaf
(Cut 3)

Note: *Add seam allowance when cutting*

Bird
(Cut 1)

Small Flower
(Cut 1)

Spring Blossom
(Cut 12)

Bird Wing
(Cut 1)

2   Arrange the fabric strips into an order that pleases you. Sew the strips together along the length and press all the seams carefully to one side.

3   Using the Large Wedge template or the 18-degree ruler, cut 10 wedges each from the Summer and Fall strips, and six wedges from the Spring. You'll find that the strip sets are wider than the length of the ruler. To begin with, set the thin end of the shape on the bottom of the strips and trim off the excess at the top, and then, when you cut the opposite shape, place the wide end of the ruler against the top of the strips and trim off the bottom excess. This ensures that the seams in the leaf pieces do not match and will make random shapes when sewn together.

4   Matching the top and bottom edges of the stripped wedges, sew together the Summer and Fall wedges to make half-circles. Press all the seams to one side.

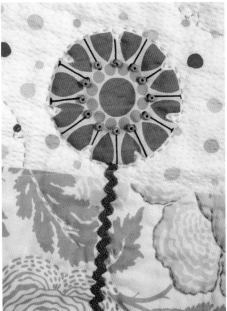

BACKGROUND BLOCKS

5   Next, sew the "ground" fabric for each season block to the bottom edge of the block background, creating a piece 21½ x 22 inches. Press the seam on this block open to reduce bulk under the appliqué.

APPLIQUÉ

Read the instructions for Appliqué on page 198 before proceeding.

6   Using the gel pen, trace around the Tree Template onto the front of each of the brown fabrics. Cut the shapes out, ¼ inch outside the line, using fabric scissors. Set aside.

7   Using the gel pen, draw a line ¼ inch in from the edge of the Spring leaf wedges. Also draw a line ¼ inch inside the edges of the Summer and Fall leaf semicircles. Finger-press along all of these lines.

TIP: *Do not clip the curves into the tree branches yet as this will cause fraying. Finger-press the curves but leave the fabric intact.*

8   Place the Summer leaves onto the Summer background and center the Tree piece on top, making sure that all the edges of the bottom of the leaf piece will be under the tree branches when they are sewn.

9   Carefully lift the edges of the fabric and apply the appliqué glue to the fabric, at least ¼ inch inside the silver line. Leave to dry for a few minutes, and then appliqué the pieces in place, using threads to match the appliqué fabrics.

10 Repeat this process with the Fall and Winter blocks. (The Winter tree has no leaves, of course, and is appliquéd directly onto the background.) For the Spring block, space the six fabric wedges out in a fan shape, allowing the background to show between them, to represent the sparse blossoms and leaves of the season.

11 Complete each block by adding the appliqué decorations in the same manner, using the leftover fabrics from the leaves and purple feature fabric. Follow the picture of the quilt for placement guidance. Summer has two Large Flowers and one Small Flower. The optional blue rickrack is used for the flower stems, or you could make bias strips instead. Fall has three Leaves falling from the tree, and Spring has 14 Spring Blossoms, using the purple feature fabric, and a little Bird with a Wing. When you have appliquéd the Bird and Wing, add legs in backstitch and a worm in stem stitch, using dark brown perle cotton.

INNER BORDERS (PIECED WEDGES)

12 There are two different lengths of Inner Border. Take the wedges you cut from the brown and purple fabrics. For the horizontal borders, start with a purple wedge and sew together 32 wedges, alternating purple

Diagram 1

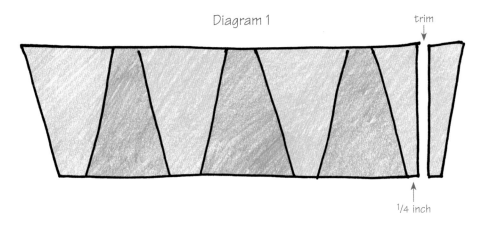

and brown as you go, and mixing the brown fabrics up well. You will end with a brown wedge. Press the seams toward the brown fabric. Make six borders like this.

13 For the vertical borders, start with a brown wedge and sew together 33 wedges, as above, ending with a brown wedge. Make six borders like this. (Keep track of which borders are which!)

14 At the beginning and end of each border strip, trim the wedge to be square by using your straight quilter's ruler and measuring ¼ inch from the seam of the last wedge (Diagram 1).

ASSEMBLING THE QUILT TOP

15 Sew a vertical Inner Border strip to the side of the Summer block, and then another vertical border to the other side. Next sew the Fall block, and then another Inner Border strip. Press. Repeat with the Winter and Spring blocks.

16 From the appliqué scraps, cut nine 2¼-inch squares of different colors. Sew a border strip that starts with a square, and then a horizontal Inner Border strip, and then a square, and then another strip, and end with another square. Make three borders like this.

17 Sew the quilt top together by sewing the horizontal borders to the top, bottom, and in between the Seasons blocks. Press the seams toward the blocks.

OUTER BORDERS (PURPLE)

18 Join all five Outer Border strips together into one long strip, first removing the selvages.

19 Measure your quilt through the center in both directions. Cut two strips to the length of the top and bottom of the quilt. Pin the middle of the strip to the middle of the top of the quilt, pin the ends, and then pin in between, easing as you go, if needed. Sew and repeat the process with the bottom strip.

20 Cut two pieces to the length of the side of the quilt. Sew a 3½-inch brown corner square to each end of both strips and attach as above. Press. Your quilt top is complete!

Backing, quilting, and binding

Cut the backing fabric crosswise in half, giving two 63-inch pieces. Remove the selvages and stitch the pieces together up the middle seam. Press the seam open and press the backing piece carefully.

Refer to pages 204–211 for instructions on finishing.

I hand-quilted The Seasons using several different perle no. 8 cottons. All the trees, flowers, and leaves are outline-quilted. I quilted twigs coming from the branches on the Winter block and quilted white parallel lines behind the trees and into the ground to make it look icy. The Summer tree is outline-quilted, and I used the Large Flower template to quilt flowers into the background around the tree. The Fall block has wavy lines quilted into the background to represent the wind, and the Spring block has circles quilted all over the background to represent blossoms. I also quilted just inside all the purple wedges in the Inner Border, and quilted windy lines and leaves, using the Leaf template, in the Outer Border.

Beading

When you have completed the quilting, you may want to attach the crystal beads to the branches of the Winter tree and add the blue beads to the Summer flowers. Do not do this if the quilt is intended for a small child.

Shared Inspiration

It's fun to collect vintage fabrics and plan wonderful projects. These two quilts make great use of vintage fabrics as center medallions, half-square triangles, and a few well-planned borders. They are combined with Japanese linen mixes as well, to compensate for the slightly heavier-weight older fabrics. It is important to plan the use of the vintage fabric at the start of a project such as this, as there is usually a limited supply.

Kismet

Calling It Curtains

Kismet

 Kathy Doughty

THE IDEA

We all do it: find a fabric that speaks to us and we have to have it. If the truth be told, a lot of these precious fabric remnants then live in closet collections as we savor the thought of what they could be. The pheasants in this vintage fabric inspired visions of the Pilgrims preparing for the first Thanksgiving in the New World, so I hung it on my design wall to enjoy. By chance, it ended up hanging next to the green fabric as I was using the red and . . . well, that's just kismet!

Half-square triangles are dynamic in borders. To make them accurately and perfectly every time, we recommend adding a 45-degree ruler to your equipment stash.

Finished quilt size

Queen, 92½ inches square

Materials and tools

3⅓ yards brown-print fabric

2 yards green-print fabric

⅞ yard gray-print fabric

⅝ yard red-print fabric for cornerstones

1⅞ yards brown-striped fabric for border

8¼ yards backing fabric

¾ yard binding fabric

99-inch-square cotton batting

Neutral-colored cotton thread for piecing

Rotary cutter, quilter's ruler, and cutting mat

Half-square (45-degree) ruler (optional)

5 balls perle cotton no. 8 for hand-quilting

NOTE: *It is recommended that all fabrics be 100 percent cotton, and be ironed. Requirements are based on fabric 44 inches wide. Unless otherwise stated, all seam allowances are ¼ inch throughout. Color test any dark fabrics that you are using (see page 189), and wash them before cutting if they run.*

Please read all instructions before starting.

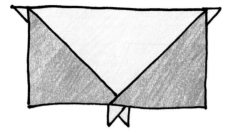

Diagram 1

Diagram 2

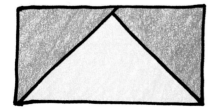

Cutting

All fabrics are strip cut across the width of the fabric from fold to selvage unless otherwise specified, or unless you are using a directional print (cut off all selvages first). Cut the largest pieces first.

FROM BROWN FABRIC, CUT:
- One 16½-inch square, for the Center Star.
- One strip, 8⅞ inches wide. Cross cut four squares, and then cross cut on the diagonal to make eight half-square triangles, for the Center Star.
- Five strips, 8½ inches wide. Sew them end to end into one long strip, and set aside for Border 3.
- Six strips, 4⅞ inches wide. Cross cut into 48 squares, and then cross cut on the diagonal, giving 96 half-square triangles, for Borders 1 and 5.

FROM GREEN FABRIC, CUT:
- Four 8½-inch squares, for the Center Medallion.
- One 17-inch square. Cross cut it on the diagonal twice to give four quarter-square triangles, for the Center Medallion.
- Five strips, 3½ inches wide. Sew together, end to end, to make one length, and set aside for Border 2.
- Six strips, 1½ inches wide. Sew together, end to end, to make one length, and set aside for Border 4.
- Seven strips, 2½ inches wide. Sew together, end to end, to make one length, and set aside for Border 6.

FROM GRAY FABRIC, CUT:
- Six strips, each 4⅞ inches wide. Cross cut into 48 squares, and then cross cut these squares on the diagonal, giving 96 half-square triangles for Borders 1 and 5.

FROM RED FABRIC, CUT:
- Two strips, 8½ inches wide. Cross cut into eight squares, for the corners of Borders 3 and 7.
- One strip, 4½ inches wide. Cross cut into eight squares, for the corners of Borders 1 and 5.

FROM BROWN–STRIPED FABRIC, CUT:
- Eight strips, 8½ inches wide. Sew them together end to end, and set aside for Border 7.

FROM BINDING FABRIC, CUT:
- Nine strips, 2½ inches wide. Join the strips, end to end, using 45-degree seams, and press seams to one side.

Constructing the quilt top

CENTER MEDALLION

1. Pin, then sew, a brown half-square triangle to each short side of a green quarter-square triangle to make a Flying Geese block (Diagram 1). Repeat to make four Flying Geese blocks in total.

2. Sew a Flying Geese block to two opposite sides of the center brown square (Diagram 2).

3. Sew two green squares to each end of the remaining two Flying Geese blocks (Diagram 3).

4. Match and pin the long edges of these sections to the center, and then sew them to complete the Center Medallion (Diagram 4).

BORDER 1 (HALF-SQUARE TRIANGLES)

5. Arrange the brown and gray half-square triangles into 96 pairs of one brown/one gray triangle.

6. Sew 32 of these half-square triangle pairs together along the diagonal edge, press open and flat. Trim the "ears." (Set the remaining 64 pairs aside for Border 5.)

7. Sew four sets of the eight half-square triangle pairs together into rows.

8. Sew one 4½-inch red square to both ends of two of these strips.

9. Join the two shorter strips to opposite sides of the Center Medallion, taking care that the brown half-square triangles point away from the center of the quilt.

10. Match and pin the remaining longer strips in the same way and sew them to form the square. The quilt top should now measure 40½ inches square. (If your measurements differ, you'll need to adapt your borders.)

BORDER 2 (GREEN)

11. From the joined Border 2 strip, cut two strips, 3½ x 40½ inches, and two strips, 3½ x 46½ inches.

12. Find the middle of one of the shorter strips and the middle of the top edge of the quilt top and pin. Match and pin the ends, and then pin the edges in between. Sew the shorter strips to the top and bottom of the quilt in this manner and press the seam in toward the center.

13. Sew the 3½ x 46½-inch green strips to the remaining sides in the same manner. The quilt top should now measure 46½ inches square.

BORDER 3 (BROWN)

14. From the joined Border 3 strip, cut four strips, each 8½ x 46½ inches.

15. Sew an 8½-inch red square to both ends of two of the strips.

16. Attach the shorter border strips to the top and bottom of the quilt top, as for Border 2, then match and sew the longer strips in the same manner. The quilt top should now measure 62½ inches square.

Diagram 3

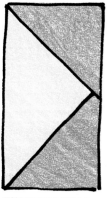

Diagram 4

BORDER 4 (GREEN)

17 From the joined Border 4 strip, cut two strips, each 1½ x 62½ inches, and two strips, each 1½ x 64½ inches.

18 Attach the border strips as for Border 2. The quilt top should now measure 64½ inches square.

BORDER 5 (HALF-SQUARE TRIANGLES)

19 Sew the remaining 64 pairs of half-square triangles together along the diagonal edge, press open and flat. Trim the ears.

20 Sew four sets of 16 half-square triangle pairs together into rows.

21 Sew one 4½-inch red square to both ends of two of these strips.

22 Attach the border strips as for Border 1, sewing the shorter strips first, followed by the longer strips, and taking care that the brown half-square triangles point away from the center of the quilt. The quilt top should now measure 72½ inches square.

BORDER 6 (GREEN)

23 From the joined Border 6 strip, cut two strips, each 2½ x 72½ inches, and two strips, each 2½ x 76½ inches.

24 Attach the border strips as for Border 2. The quilt top should now measure 76½ inches square.

BORDER 7 (BROWN STRIPE)

25 From the joined Border 7 strip, cut four strips, each 8½ x 76½ inches.

26 Sew an 8½-inch red square to both ends of two of the border strips.

27 Attach the border strips as for Border 3, sewing the shorter strips first. Your quilt top is complete!

Backing, quilting, and binding

Cut the backing fabric crosswise into three pieces, each 99 inches long. Remove the selvages and sew the lengths together to form one backing piece. Press the seams open.

Refer to pages 204–211 for instructions on finishing.

Kismet was hand-quilted using perle cotton no. 8 in brown and green. The Center Medallion and vintage borders have diagonal lines repeated throughout in brown at 2-inch intervals. The green Japanese linen simply begged to be quilted with a vine pattern to echo the design of the fabric: the green quilting lines weave randomly through the borders with vines and leaves. The half-square triangle borders are quilted to echo the seam lines. The outside border of the quilt is where we often find the most tugging and pulling, so I quilted heavily alongside the stripes to give the quilt strength.

Calling It Curtains

 Sarah Fielke

THE IDEA

We are constantly setting challenges for our students, and for our quilting group, the Cut Loose Quilters, in particular. As soon as we give them a challenge we think will keep them busy, they come back with a finished quilt top. One day in class, however, they set *us* a challenge! Everyone in the class, teachers included, was given a piece of a vintage curtain. Over the coming weeks, we saw skirts and bags and pin cushions . . . and Calling It Curtains. The fabric was a bit of a puzzle to begin with, as the color combination was very vintage, until I saw the lovely clear blues and bold purple in the flowers, and the deep olive green in the leaves. A little rummaging through the stash (and a bit of cursing about the limited supply of some things), and the palette was born.

Finished quilt size
Throw, 68½ inches square

Materials and tools
Large piece vintage fabric or ⅞ yard patchwork fabric with a large motif for Center Medallion and Borders 1 and 7
3 yards brown linen for Borders 2, 4, 6, and 7
1¼ yards purple-spotted fabric for borders
⅔ yard blue-patterned fabric for borders and appliqué
¾ yard green-patterned linen for borders and appliqué
⅝ yard blue-and-orange-spotted fabric for binding
⅝ yard double-sided appliqué webbing for appliqué
4⅛ yards spotted fabric for backing
75-inch square cotton batting
Rotary cutter, quilter's ruler, and cutting mat
Neutral-colored cotton thread for piecing
Template plastic and 2B pencil
Machine thread for machine blanket stitch, to match appliqué fabrics

NOTE: *It is recommended that all fabrics be 100 percent cotton, and be ironed. Requirements are based on fabric 44 inches wide. Unless otherwise stated, all seam allowances are ¼ inch throughout. Color test any dark fabrics that you are using (see page 189), and wash them before cutting if they run. This quilt was made using several linen fabrics, which are more loosely woven than patchwork cotton. Due to the loosely woven nature of linen, be careful when cutting and pressing that you do not distort the fabrics.*

Please read all instructions before starting.

Template

Trace the appliqué shape for the Berry (page 49) onto template plastic and cut out accurately with sharp scissors–not fabric scissors!

Cutting

All fabrics are strip cut across the width of the fabric from fold to selvage unless otherwise specified or unless you are using a directional print (cut off all selvages first). Cut the largest pieces first.

FROM VINTAGE FABRIC (OR MEDALLION FABRIC), CUT:

- One square, 22½ inches, for the center.
- 24 squares, each 2⅞ inches. Cut these squares in half on the diagonal to yield 48 half-square triangles for Border 1.
- Four squares, each 2½ inches, for the cornerstones in Border 7.

FROM BROWN LINEN, CUT:

- Four strips, 4½ inches wide, for Border 2.
- Six strips, 2½ inches wide. Cross cut to yield 84 squares, each 2½ inches, for Border 4.
- Seven strips, 7½ inches wide, for Border 6.
- Five strips, 2⅞ inches wide. Cross cut 64 squares, each 2⅞ inches. Cut these squares on the diagonal to yield 128 half-square triangles for Border 7.

FROM PURPLE-SPOTTED FABRIC, CUT:

- 14 strips, 2⅞ inches wide. Cross cut into 172 squares, each 2⅞ inches. Cut these squares on the diagonal to yield 344 half-square triangles for borders as follows: 48 for Border 1, 72 for Border 3, 96 for Border 5, and 128 for Border 7.

FROM BLUE-PATTERNED FABRIC, CUT:

- Six strips, 2½ inches wide. Cross cut to yield 84 squares, each 2½ inches, for Border 4.
- One strip, 4½ inches wide. Cross cut to yield four squares, each 4½ inches, for the cornerstones of Border 2.
- The remaining fabric is for the Berries in the appliqué of Border 6. Using your template, trace 72 Berries onto the paper side of the appliqué webbing. Cut the Berries out roughly and iron them, glue-side down, onto the wrong side of the fabric. Cut the Berries out accurately on the traced line, using scissors.

Diagram 1

FROM GREEN-PATTERNED LINEN, CUT:

- Seven strips, 2⅞ inches wide. Cross cut to yield 84 squares, each 2⅞ inches. Cross cut these squares to yield 168 half-square triangles for borders as follows: 72 for Border 3 and 96 for Border 5.
- The remaining fabric is for the appliqué in Border 6. Cut a piece of appliqué webbing, about 6 x 25 inches. Iron this piece, as a whole, onto the wrong side of the green-patterned linen. From this piece, using a rotary cutter, cut 24 rectangles, each 1 x 5½ inches, for the Stems.

FROM BINDING FABRIC, CUT:

- Eight strips, 2½ inches wide. Join the strips, end to end, using 45-degree seams, and press seams to one side.

Constructing the quilt top

BORDER 1 (HALF-SQUARE TRIANGLES)

1 Take the 48 vintage fabric and 48 purple-spotted half-square triangles for Border 1 and sew them into alternating pairs along the diagonal edge to form 48 squares (Diagram 1).

2 Using the photograph as a guide for the direction of the triangles, piece two strips of 11 squares each, and two strips of 13 squares each.

3 Find the middle of one of the shorter strips and the middle of the top edge of the Center Medallion and pin. Match and pin the ends, and pin the edges in between. Sew the shorter strips to the top and bottom of the Center Medallion in this manner and press the seams toward the center.

4 Next, sew the longer strips to either side of the Center Medallion, taking care to match the seams on the corners. Press.

BORDER 2 (BROWN LINEN)

5 Measure your quilt top through the center. It should now measure 26½ inches square. Trim the brown linen 4½-inch border strips to yield four pieces, each 4½ x 26½ inches (or your measurement).

6 Find the center of one of the brown linen strips and pin to the quilt top, as for Border 1, and then sew the strip to the quilt top. Repeat for the opposite side of the quilt top.

7 Sew a blue-patterned square to each end of the two remaining brown linen strips. Attach to the quilt top as for Border 1, taking care to match the seams at the corners. Measure the quilt top through the center in both directions. It should now measure 34½ inches square.

BORDER 3 (HALF-SQUARE TRIANGLES)

8 Take the 72 purple-spotted and 72 green-patterned half-square triangles for Border 3 and sew them into alternating pairs along the diagonal edge to form 72 squares.

Diagram 2

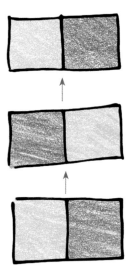

9   Using the photograph as a guide for the direction of the triangles, piece two strips of 17 squares each, and two strips of 19 squares each.

10 Pinning as for Border 1, sew the shorter strips to the top and bottom of the quilt top and press the seam inward toward the center panel.

11 Next, sew the longer strips to either side of the quilt top, taking care to match the seams on the corners. Press. Measure the quilt top through the center in both directions. Your top should now measure 38½ inches square.

BORDER 4 (CHECKERBOARD)

12 Take the 84 brown linen and the 84 blue-patterned squares for Border 4 and sew them into 84 alternating pairs. Sew the pairs, checkerboard fashion (Diagram 2), into two rows of 19 pairs and two rows of 23 pairs, taking care to watch that the checkerboard pattern will follow in correct sequence around the corners.

13 Pinning as for the previous borders, sew the shorter strips to the top and bottom of the quilt top. Press.

14 Next, sew the longer strips to either side of the quilt top, matching the seams at the corners. Press. Measure the quilt top through the center in both directions. It should now measure 46½ inches square.

BORDER 5 (HALF-SQUARE TRIANGLES)

15 Take the 96 purple-spotted and 96 green-patterned half-square triangles for Border 5 and sew them into alternating pairs along the diagonal edge to form 96 squares.

16 Using the photograph as a guide for the direction of the triangles, piece two strips of 23 squares each, and two strips of 25 squares each.

17 Pinning as for the previous borders, sew the shorter strips to the top and bottom of the quilt top and press the seam in toward the Center Medallion.

18 Next, sew the longer strips to either side of the quilt top, taking care to match the seams on the corners. Press. Measure the quilt through the center in both directions to ensure it is square. It should now measure 50½ inches square.

BORDER 6 (BROWN LINEN)

19 Trim four of the 7½-inch-wide brown linen strips to 42 inches long. From the fifth strip, cut two pieces, each 9 inches long, and sew one to the end of two 42-inch strips, giving two strips, each 50½ inches long (or the measurement of your quilt top).

20 From the remaining two 7½-inch-wide brown linen strips, cut two pieces, each 25 inches long. Sew one to each of the remaining two 42-inch pieces, creating two pieces, each 66½ inches long. Press. Do not attach borders until appliqué is complete.

APPLIQUÉ

21 Find the center of one of the brown border strips and mark with a pin or a piece of chalk. Measure 12 inches to the right and mark the place, and then 12 inches to the left and do the same. Remove the backing paper from the back of one of the green Stem rectangles, and center the Stem, right side up, over the center mark, lining the bottom of the Stem up with the edge of the border piece. Iron the Stem to the border piece. Do the same with the left- and right-hand marks you made.

22 Center a Berry over the top of each Stem, and one to the right and left of each. Refer to the photograph for placement. Iron the Berries down.

23 Set your sewing machine to a blanket stitch with a stitch length of about 1.5 and a width of 2. Using a matching thread, blanket-stitch the Berries and Stems down. Alternately, you could use a zigzag stitch or hand blanket-stitch your appliqué. Repeat these steps for the appliqué on all four borders.

24 Pinning as for the previous borders, sew the short strips to the top and bottom of the quilt top. Press. Sew the longer strips to the sides of the quilt top in the same manner and press.

25 Unpick the seam at the inner corner of the border, about 2 inches in each direction. Position a Stem piece at 90 degrees to each corner, and one at 45 degrees over the top. Cut the middle Stem into a "v" shape at the bottom to allow for pressing (Diagram 3). Iron the pieces down, and then re-sew the border to the quilt top, trapping the edges in the seam. Position the Berries as before and blanket-stitch in place. Repeat on all four corners and press.

Diagram 3

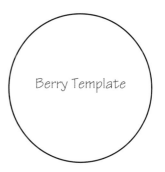

Berry Template

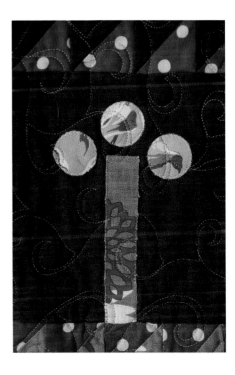

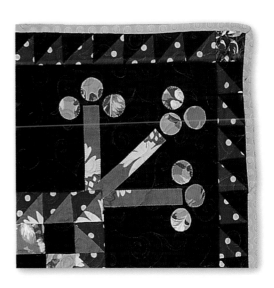

BORDER 7 (HALF–SQUARE TRIANGLES)

26 Take the 128 purple-spotted and 128 brown linen half-square triangles for Border 7 and sew them into pairs along the diagonal edge to form 128 squares. Using the photograph as a guide for the direction of the triangles, piece four strips of 32 squares each.

27 Sew a 2½-inch vintage fabric square to either end of two of the strips.

28 Pinning as for the previous borders, sew the shorter strips to the top and bottom of the quilt top, and press the seam in toward the Center Medallion.

29 Next, sew the longer strips to either side of the quilt, taking care to match the seams on the corners. Press. Your quilt top is complete!

Backing, quilting, and binding

Cut the backing fabric crosswise in half, giving two 74-inch pieces. Remove the selvages and stitch the pieces together up the middle seam. Press the seam open and press the backing piece carefully.

Refer to pages 204–211 for instructions on finishing.

I machine-quilted Calling It Curtains in an all-over spiral pattern, using blue thread. The curling spirals echo the leafy fronds in the center panel and provide a nice texture in the large, plain borders.

Shared Inspiration

~ ~ ~ ~ ~

Repeating a block throughout a quilt creates a sense of directional movement. The same block often looks completely different, depending on the colors that set the mood, and the placement or size of the blocks. Both of these quilts use a Flying Geese motif— pieced in different ways, repeated throughout the quilt, and coming from a central square—for a very different and dynamic effect.

Playground Days

Jungle Boogie

Playground Days

 Kathy Doughty

THE IDEA

Simple blocks appeal to me when I need immediate satisfaction. The rhythm of the repetition is soothing as the blocks whiz through the machine and something takes shape rather quickly. The two standard repeat blocks, half-square triangles (so easy with a half-square ruler) and the nine patch, can both be combined in a mind-boggling array of patterns.

This quilt uses fabric from Denyse Schmidt's "Katie Jump Rope" range. It is a reminder of those carefree days skipping on a playground somewhere. The corners are made with a Sunburst Kit from Marti Michell. I encourage you to try this fun ruler kit to make these corners. . . . Come on, there are only four and you can do it by hand or on the machine easily!

Finished quilt size
Double bed, 78½ x 91½ inches
Block size: 14 inches, including seam allowance

Materials and tools
4⅜ yards white quilter's muslin
4⅓ yards in total of various patterned fabrics (a minimum of 12 inches per fabric)
¾ yard binding fabric
5½ yards backing fabric
95 x 98 inches cotton batting
Neutral-colored cotton thread for piecing
Rotary cutter, quilter's ruler, and cutting mat
Half-square ruler (optional, but recommended for accuracy)
Marti Michell Sunburst Block Kit Set F (optional, for Sunburst corner blocks)

NOTE: *It is recommended that all fabrics be 100 percent cotton, and be ironed. Requirements are based on fabric 44 inches wide. Unless otherwise stated, all seam allowances are ¼ inch throughout. Color test any dark fabrics that you are using (see page 189), and wash them before cutting if they run.*

   Please read all instructions before starting.

Diagram 1

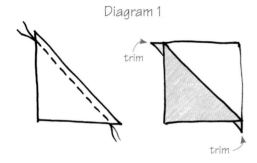

Diagram 2

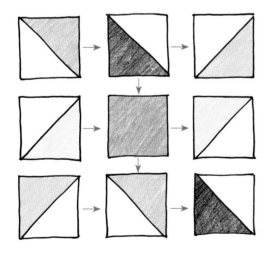

Cutting

All fabrics are strip cut across the width of the fabric from fold to selvage unless otherwise specified or unless you are using a directional print (cut off all selvages first). Cut the largest pieces first. It is advisable, when starting a new project, to make one complete block first, to ensure all the measurements are right before cutting all the fabric.

FROM WHITE FABRIC, CUT:

- 18 strips, 2 inches wide, for nine-patch blocks in the border.
- Two strips, 13½ inches wide. Cross cut into four squares, each 13½ inches, for the corners. (These will be trimmed to 12½ inches.)

If you are using the half-square ruler, cut:

- 10 strips, 5 inches wide. Set aside to make half-square triangles later.

If you are not using the half-square ruler, cut:

- 12 strips, 5⅜ inches wide. Cross cut into 80 squares.

FROM PATTERNED FABRICS, CUT:

- Six strips, 5 inches wide. Cross cut into 48 squares.
- 18 strips, 2 inches wide, for nine-patch blocks in the border.
- Six strips, 3½ inches wide. Cross cut into 18 rectangles, each 3½ x 14 inches, for the borders.

If you are using the half-square ruler, cut:

- 10 strips, 5 inches wide. Set aside to make half-square triangles later.

If you are not using the half-square ruler, cut:

- 12 strips, 5⅜ inches wide. Cross cut into 80 squares.

FROM BINDING FABRIC, CUT:

- Nine strips, 2½ inches wide. Join the strips, end to end, using 45-degree seams, and press seams to one side.

Constructing the quilt top

PINWHEEL BLOCKS (MAKE 20)

1 *If you are using the half-square ruler:* Match a white 5-inch strip to a patterned 5-inch strip, with right sides together. Using the ruler, and turning it after each cut, cross cut the double strip diagonally to make 16 half-square triangle pairs. Repeat for the remaining strips, to give 160 half-square triangle pairs in all.

2 *If you are not using the ruler:* Match one white and one patterned 5⅜-inch square, right sides together. Cross cut on the diagonal, and repeat with the remaining squares to make 160 half-square triangle pairs.

3 Sew along the diagonal of the half-square triangle pairs to make 160 half-square triangle squares (Diagram 1). Press seams to the dark side, and trim the "ears," if applicable.

4   Set out the half-square triangle squares in sets of eight, with a solid
    5-inch square in the center (Diagram 2). Be sure to check that the
    diagonal seams are going as pictured, to form the pinwheel pattern.
    Sew into horizontal rows and then into blocks. Make 20 blocks in this
    manner. The pictured blocks are divided into loosely alternating warm
    colors or cool colors.

ASSEMBLING THE PINWHEEL BLOCKS

The body of the quilt is five rows of four blocks, alternating warm and cool
colors for effect. Lay the blocks out on the floor or, preferably, on a design
wall (see page 202), for color balancing.

5   Number each row from top to bottom and sew the first block to the
    second block for all rows. Leave all connecting threads uncut until
    you are finished with all rows. Now sew block two to block three
    for all rows. Do this until the quilt rows are assembled, and then sew
    the first row to the second, the second to the third, and so on until
    finished. The top should now measure 54½ x 68 inches, including
    seam allowance.

NINE-PATCH BLOCKS (MAKE 80)

6   Set two 2-inch printed strips with one white strip of the same width.
    Sew them together with the white in the middle. Repeat with two white
    strips and one printed strip. Press the seams to the dark side in either
    case. Be careful not to stretch the strips in any direction.
7   Cross cut these pieced strips into 2-inch-wide strips (Diagram 3).
8   Sew these sets together in alternating patterns until you have
    80 nine-patch blocks (Diagram 4). Each nine-patch block should
    measure 5 inches square, including seam allowance.

SUNBURST BLOCKS, OPTIONAL (MAKE 4)

If you do not wish to make the Sunburst blocks, you can leave the corner
squares blank. Simply trim the corner squares to 12½ inches square and
proceed with the borders.

9   Using scraps from the body of the quilt, make four Sunburst blocks,
    following the instructions in the Marti Michell Sunburst Block kit.
10 To appliqué the completed Sunburst blocks to the white 13½-inch
    squares, fold the white squares in half and in half again, and finger-
    press the corners. Do the same for the Sunburst block and match the
    creases, pin, and then needle-turn appliqué (see page 198) the top
    to the square. Trim the blocks to 12½ inches square.

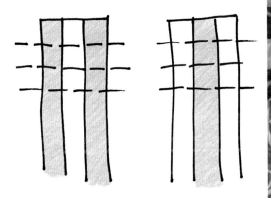

Diagram 3

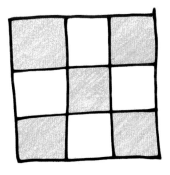

Diagram 4

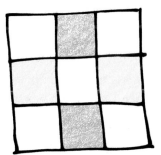

Diagram 5

11 Measure the width and length of the quilt through the middle and note these measurements. When you are sewing the border strips, check to be sure the measurements match.

12 Using the photograph as a guide, lay out the nine-patch blocks, alternating them with the solid 5-inch squares, as shown (Diagram 5). Sew them together in long strips (four rows of 12 squares for the top and bottom borders, and four rows of 15 squares for the sides). Matching the seams carefully, sew the rows together into four nine-patch borders.

13 Sewing end to end, piece together two rows of five and two rows of four 3½ x 14-inch rectangles for the outer borders.

14 Matching both middles and ends of the nine-patch and rectangle borders, sew them together.

15 Sew a white square (with or without the Sunburst appliqué) to both ends of the top and bottom borders.

16 Fold the side border strips in half and press a crease in the center. Match the crease to the center of the quilt top, pin, and then pin the two ends to the ends of the quilt top. Pin securely along the sides of the quilt top to ensure the two pieces are equal. Sew together.

17 Repeat this process for the top and bottom borders. Your quilt top is complete!

Backing, quilting, and binding

Cut the backing fabric crosswise in half, giving two lengths, each 99 inches long. Remove the selvages and sew the lengths together to form one backing piece. Press the seam allowance open.

Refer to pages 204–211 for instructions on finishing.

Playground Days was commercially machine-quilted in white cotton. It would be suited to hand-quilting in straight lines as well. Playground Days is just that—a quilt that evokes the feeling of running on the playground as a child. So when I selected a pattern for machine-quilting, I looked for one that had lots of flowing, breezy lines, such as pinwheels or kites.

Jungle Boogie

 Sarah Fielke

THE IDEA

This quilt was made for my son, Oscar, who grooves on his tuba to the jungle beat. He picked out the panther fabric and I picked blacks, greens, and a block that would look like cats' paws padding through the undergrowth.

This quilt is not difficult to make, since you use a clever technique to make four Flying Geese at once and do not have to cut any triangles. You could also use a Flying Geese ruler if you prefer, to make cutting your units more accurate.

Finished quilt size

King single, 67 x 96 inches
Block size: 19½ inches, including seam allowance

Materials and tools

1 yard green-and-black striped fabric for block centers and binding
⅔ yard green-and-black-patterned fabric for block corners
1⅔ yards red-and-tan-spotted fabric
1⅔ yards tan-and-red-spotted fabric (reverse)
½ yard each of two different black tone-on-tone prints, and
    ⅔ yard extra of one (1⅔ yards fabric in total)
¼ yard each of 14 different green fabrics (3½ yards
    fabric in total)
5⅔ yards backing fabric
75 x 102 inches cotton batting
2B pencil
Quarter-inch ruler
Rotary cutter, quilter's ruler, and cutting mat
Neutral-colored cotton thread for piecing

NOTE: *It is recommended that all fabrics be 100 percent cotton, and be ironed. Requirements are based on fabric 44 inches wide. Unless otherwise stated, all seam allowances are ¼ inch throughout. Color test any dark fabrics that you are using (see page 189), and wash them before cutting if they run.*
  Please read all instructions before starting.

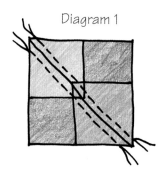

Diagram 1

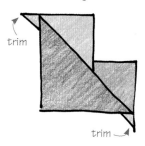

Diagram 2

Diagram 3

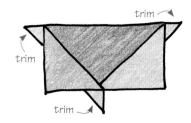

Diagram 4

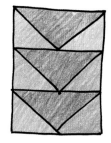

Diagram 5

Cutting

All fabrics are strip cut across the width of the fabric from fold to selvage unless otherwise specified, or unless you are using a directional print (cut off all selvages first). Cut the largest pieces first.

FROM GREEN-AND-BLACK-STRIPED FABRIC, CUT:

- Two strips, 5 inches wide. Cross cut into 15 squares, each 5 inches, for block centers.
- Nine strips, 2½ inches wide, for the binding. Join the strips, end to end, using 45-degree seams, and press seams to one side.

FROM BLACK-AND-GREEN-PATTERNED FABRIC, CUT:

- Six strips, 3½ inches wide. Cross cut into 60 squares, each 3½ inches, for the block corners.

FROM RED-AND-TAN-SPOTTED FABRIC, CUT:

- Four strips, 14½ inches wide. Cross cut into eight squares, each 14½ inches. When you are ready to piece, cross cut these squares across both diagonals into 32 quarter-square triangles.

FROM TAN-AND-RED-SPOTTED FABRIC, CUT:

- Four strips, 14½ inches wide. Cross cut into eight squares, each 14½ inches. When you are ready to piece, cross cut these squares across both diagonals into 32 quarter-square triangles.

FROM THE SMALLER PIECE OF BLACK FABRIC, CUT:

- Three strips, 5½ inches wide. Cross cut these strips into 21 squares, each 5½ inches.

FROM THE LARGER PIECE OF BLACK FABRIC, CUT:

- Seven strips, 5½ inches wide. Cross cut into 5½-inch squares, until you have a total of 66 black squares (including the previous 21).

FROM EACH OF 14 GREEN FABRICS, CUT:

- Two strips, 3⅛ inches wide, for a total of 28 strips. Cross cut these strips until you have 324 squares, each 3⅛ inches.

Constructing the quilt top

There are 15 blocks, called Road to California, laid out in Flying Geese style. You may want to make just one of the Flying Geese units first, so that you get used to the technique before you start any chain-piecing or quick sewing. This technique will give you four very accurate Flying Geese units from one square, eliminating the need for working with bias.

FLYING GEESE UNITS

1 Begin by laying two green 3⅛-inch squares on top of a black 5½-inch square, putting a green square facedown on two diagonal corners of the black square. Rule three pencil lines onto the green squares—one straight up the diagonal corners of the squares, and the remaining two ¼ inch on either side (Diagram 1). The center line is your cutting line and the two lines on either side are your sewing lines.

2 Before cutting, sew along the sewing lines, through all layers, and then cut apart on the center cutting line. Finger-press the triangles away from the black fabric (Diagram 2).

3 Now place a green square in the corner of the resulting black triangles, and rule your three lines as before (Diagram 3). Sew along the sewing lines, and then cut apart on the center cutting line and press. You should have four Flying Geese units (Diagram 4).

4 Repeat Steps 1 to 3 until you have made 264 Flying Geese units.

5 Sew the Flying Geese together into 60 units of three Flying Geese each (Diagram 5). The remaining 84 Flying Geese units are for the borders, and the remaining 60 green squares are for the block corner pieces.

BLOCK CORNER UNITS

6 Cut the remaining 60 green squares in half on the diagonal, creating 120 half-square triangles.

7 Sew a half-square triangle to two adjacent sides of a green-and-black-patterned corner square until you have made 60 corner units (Diagram 6).

ASSEMBLING THE BLOCKS

8 Sew a corner unit to the black end of a Flying Geese unit (Diagram 7). Press. Repeat for all 60 units of each.

9 Sew a Flying Geese/Corner unit to either side of the 15 green-and-black-striped 5-inch block centers (Diagram 8, page 64). Make 15.

10 Lay the remaining pieces of the block out next to the sewing machine, reversing the position of the spotted fabrics, as shown in the photograph. (You'll have two quarter-square triangles in each fabric left over.)

11 Sew a red-and-tan triangle to one side of a Flying Geese unit, and a tan-and-red triangle to the other side. Press carefully and repeat in the opposite order for the other side of the block.

12 Sew the block together up the diagonal seams (Diagram 9, page 64). Press. Repeat Steps 11 and 12 until you have 15 blocks, each measuring 19½ inches square.

13 Sew the blocks into five rows of three across the quilt. Press the seams carefully, and then sew the five rows together. The quilt top should now measure 57½ x 95½ inches.

Diagram 6

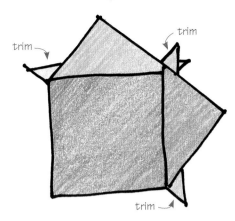

Diagram 7

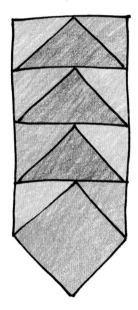

Diagram 8

Diagram 9

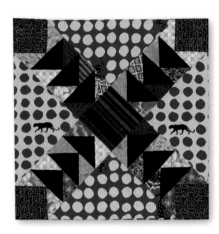

BORDER

14 Take the remaining Flying Geese units you made and sew them together into two rows of 42 Flying Geese each.

15 Find the center of one of the strips and the center of the side of the quilt top and pin. Next, match and pin the ends, and then pin in between, easing as you go, if necessary. Sew and repeat with the other side border. Your quilt top is complete!

Backing, quilting, and binding

Cut the backing fabric crosswise in half into two 103-inch pieces. Remove the selvages and stitch the pieces together up the middle seam. Press the seam allowance open and press the backing piece carefully.

Refer to pages 204–211 for instructions on finishing.

Jungle Boogie was machine-quilted using a tan thread to match the linen background of the black panther fabric. The quilter used a leafy pattern to continue the jungle theme.

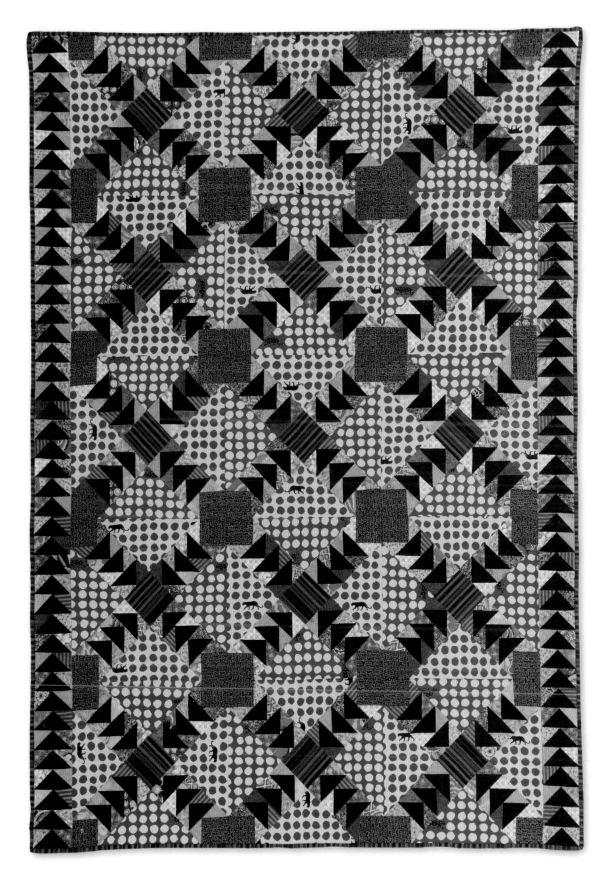

Shared Inspiration

We love looking at old quilt photos in books and vintage quilt tops for inspiration. These two projects both spring from quilts that existed before, but each one has been updated in its use of color, and by adding a bit of extra appliqué. Now & Then came from a black-and-white photo, so it is hard to imagine what the original colors were. Charlotte Sometimes was originally dark green and pale green, in plain, unpatterned fabrics.

Now & Then

Charlotte Sometimes

Now & Then

 Kathy Doughty

THE IDEA

On a retreat with quilting friends, we all threw our fabric scraps into a big pile for everyone to use. My original plan was to recreate an antique quilt that I had seen in a black-and-white photo. I selected my most treasured fabrics and, as the squares were coming together, a friend noted that this quilt was looking a bit, *ahem*, structured and organized for my style. In shocked horror, I immediately started to add interest from the scrap pile.

The end result is a collection of soft, contemporary, bright fabrics and flowers made from the scrappy discards of my treasured friends, the Cut Loose Quilters. To further break the rules, the center panel is appliquéd onto the reverse of the fabric to soften the impact.

Finished quilt size

Double bed, 78 inches square

Materials and tools

4⅜ yards background fabric

1⅔ yards in total of a variety of cool, bright fabrics for small squares

1⅔ yards in total of a variety of warm fabrics for small squares

½ yard in total of a variety of dark scrap strips, at least 2 inches wide

⅞ yard in total of a variety of scraps in reproduction colors
    for appliqué flowers

⅓ yard green scraps for leaves and stems of flowers

⅔ yard binding fabric

85-inch-square wool batting

5½ yards backing fabric

Rotary cutter, quilter's ruler, and cutting mat

Quarter-square ruler (optional)

Neutral-colored cotton thread for piecing

Template plastic

Silver gel pen

2B pencil

Appliqué pins or glue

Appliqué needles and thread to match flowers and leaves

3 balls plum perle cotton no. 8 for quilting

NOTE: *It is recommended that all fabrics be 100 percent cotton, and be ironed. Requirements are based on fabric 44 inches wide. Unless otherwise stated, all seam allowances are ¼ inch throughout. Color test any dark fabrics that you are using (see page 189), and wash them before cutting if they run.*

Please read all instructions before starting.

Templates

The appliqué shapes for both the Small and Large Flowers (Center, Outer Petals, Stem, and Leaf) are on the pattern sheet. Trace them onto template plastic, label them, and cut them out accurately.

Cutting

All fabrics are strip cut across the width of the fabric from fold to selvage unless otherwise specified or unless you are using a directional print (cut off all selvages first). Cut the largest pieces first.

FROM BACKGROUND FABRIC, CUT:

- One 22½-inch square, for the Center Medallion. (I cut this from a lightly striped fabric and then used the reverse side of it to tone down the colors. You may try this or use the background fabric you have selected. The background fabric requirements include this square.)
- Three squares, each 25½ inches. Cross cut them on the diagonal, and then again on the opposite diagonal, to make 12 quarter-square triangles for the appliquéd corners.
- Three squares, each 18½ inches. Cross cut them on the diagonal, and then again, as before, to make 12 quarter-square triangles (four for Unit 2 and eight for the side setting triangles).

FROM COOL AND WARM FABRICS, CUT:

- 46 strips, 2½ inches wide (23 strips from warm fabrics, and 23 strips from cool, bright fabrics) for the pieced blocks. Cross cut these strips into 504 squares and keep them in two separate warm and cool piles.

FROM DARK SCRAP FABRICS, CUT:

- 2-inch-wide strips for the edge triangles. These fabrics must contrast with the squares. Cross cut, using the 45-degree angle of your ruler. Space out 3¾ inches along the bottom straight grain edge of the fabric and cross cut in the opposite direction to form a triangle. Repeat with the straight grain on the top edge. Alternately, if you have a quarter-square ruler, use the 1¾-inch width for the strip and cross cut triangles in groups of six per color. You need 144 triangles in total.

FROM BINDING FABRIC, CUT:

- Eight strips, 2½ inches wide. Join the strips, end to end, using 45-degree seams, and press seams to one side.

APPLIQUÉ FABRICS

The flowers are cut from randomly sewn scrap bits. Start by sewing bits of scraps together to form a piece big enough to cover the templates, plus

¼-inch seam allowance. Trace around the edge of the templates onto the pieced scrap bits with a gel pen. Cut out the shapes with ¼-inch seam allowance outside the gel pen line.

FOR EACH OF THE 12 SMALLER FLOWERS, CUT:

- One Small Center (A), two Small Outer Petals (B and BR: flip the B template for the BR pieces), one Small Stem, and one Small Leaf, flipping the templates for half the Stem pieces so that six of your flowers will face the opposite way.

FOR THE LARGER CENTER FLOWER, CUT:

- One Large Center (A), two Large Outer Petals (B and BR: flip the B template for the BR piece), one Large Stem, and one Large Leaf.

Constructing the quilt top

APPLIQUÉ

Read the instructions for Appliqué on page 198 before proceeding.

1 Using pins or appliqué glue, center the large flower pieces, leaves, and stem on the Center Medallion, using the photograph as a guide to placement. Following the instructions for needle-turn appliqué on page 198, appliqué the pieces in place.

2 Repeat this process for each of the smaller flowers, appliquéing a smaller flower onto each of the 12 corner triangles.

UNIT 1 (MAKE 24)

3 Sew the small squares together, alternating between the separated piles of warm and cool. Make strips of six, five, four, three, two, and one. End each strip with a dark quarter-square triangle. Sew them together in descending order, being sure to match points (Diagram 1). Make 24.

UNIT 2 (MAKE 4)

4 Sew a Unit 1 to a smaller background quarter-square triangle to form a square (Diagram 2). Make four.

UNIT 3 (MAKE 8)

5 Sew a Unit 1 to both short sides of an appliquéd corner triangle (Diagram 3). Make eight.

UNIT 4 (MAKE 4)

6 Sew a smaller background setting triangle to both sides of a Unit 3 section (Diagram 4, page 72). Make four.

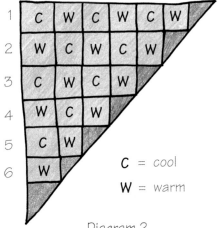

Diagram 1
Unit 1 (make 24)

C = cool
W = warm

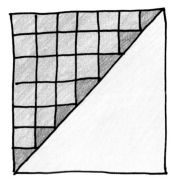

Diagram 2
Unit 2 (make 4)

Diagram 3
Unit 3 (make 8)

Diagram 4
Unit 4 (make 4)

CENTER MEDALLION

7 Match the middle of one side of the square Center Medallion with the middle of the long side of a Unit 1 section. Pin, and then sew, the unit to the medallion, and then sew another three Unit 1 sections to the remaining sides of the medallion and set on point.

ASSEMBLING THE UNITS

8 Following the Quilt Assembly Diagram, join a Unit 3 section to opposite sides of the quilt top.

9 Join a Unit 2 section to both sides of the remaining two Unit 3 sections.

10 Matching the seams, sew these longer sections to the remaining sides of the quilt top.

11 Matching center points and seams, join the four Unit 4 sections to the sides of the quilt top.

12 The final corners are the remaining four appliquéd corner triangles. Fold them in half to find the middle of the long side of the triangle and then match the center to the middle of the Unit 4 sections of the quilt top. Sew in place. Your quilt top is complete!

Backing, quilting, and binding

Cut the backing fabric crosswise in half, giving two 99-inch pieces. Remove the selvages and stitch the pieces together up the middle seam. Press the seam open and press the backing piece carefully.

Refer to pages 204–211 for instructions on finishing.

Now & Then is hand-quilted with plum perle cotton no. 8. The pieced triangles are quilted along the seams, and the solid setting triangles are quilted in a 2-inch grid. The appliquéd blocks are quilted in radiating lines around the flowers. The quilting on the Center Medallion echoes the striped fabric used for the background, and each of the appliquéd flowers is quilted along the seams of the flower petals.

Quilt Assembly Diagram

Charlotte Sometimes

 Sarah Fielke

THE IDEA

I collect old quilts and one—a vintage top, signed "Charlotte Tompkins, 1939"—was the inspiration for this quilt. I bought it because I have always wanted to make a Burgoyne Surrounded quilt, but also for the funky appliqué flowers! I enjoyed the original quilt so much that I decided to make another. The black background just seemed to attract my Kaffe Fassett stash like a magnet, the black making the saturated colors glow and flash, and the appliquéd circles creating positives and negatives around the circular piecing in the block. There are lots of small pieces and the appliqué is a bit tricky, but don't be intimidated—I bet you'll be as charmed by Charlotte's design as I was.

Finished quilt size

Double bed, 77 x 95 inches
Block size: 15½ inches, including seam allowance

Materials and tools

6⅛ yards black-patterned fabric for background
⅝ yard crimson fabric for blocks
⅝ yard orange-print fabric for blocks
6 inches orange-spotted fabric for blocks
½ yard green fabric for blocks
¼ yard each of at least twelve different prints for appliqué (this is more fabric than required, but the extra prints are needed for a scrappy look)
⅔ yard pink-and-red-patterned fabric for binding
5⅔ yards backing fabric
83 x 102 inches cotton batting
Rotary cutter, quilter's ruler, and cutting mat
Neutral-colored cotton thread for piecing
Template plastic
Silver gel pen (optional)
2B pencil
Appliqué needles
Appliqué pins or glue
Cotton sewing thread to match appliqué fabrics
Gray perle cotton no. 8 for quilting

NOTE: *It is recommended that all fabrics be 100 percent cotton, and be ironed. Requirements are based on fabric 44 inches wide. Unless otherwise stated, all seam allowances are ¼ inch throughout. Color test any dark fabrics that you are using (see page 189), and wash them before cutting if they run.*
   Please read all instructions before starting.

Templates

The appliqué shapes are printed on the pattern sheet. Trace the Flower, Tree, Circle, and Corner Tree onto template plastic and cut out accurately.

Cutting

All fabrics are strip cut across the width of the fabric from fold to selvage unless otherwise specified or unless you are using a directional print (cut off all selvages first). Cut the largest pieces first.

FROM BLACK-PATTERNED FABRIC, CUT:

- Four strips, 1½ inches wide, for Unit 1.
- Eight strips, 2½ inches wide, for Unit 2.
- Eight strips, 1½ inches wide, for Unit 3.
- 14 strips, 1½ inches wide, for Unit 4.
- Seven strips, 3½ inches wide, for Unit 5.
- Two strips, 2½ inches wide, and two strips, 1½ inches wide, for Unit 6.
- Three strips, 15½ inches wide. Cross cut these strips into 31 pieces, each 3½ x 15½ inches, for sashing.
- From the remaining fabric, remove the selvage and cut four strips, 10½ x 80 inches, along the length, for borders.

FROM CRIMSON FABRIC, CUT:

- Two strips, 1½ inches wide, for Unit 1.
- Six strips, 1½ inches wide, for Unit 4.
- Two strips, 2½ inches wide, for Unit 6.

FROM ORANGE-PRINT FABRIC, CUT:

- Two strips, 1½ inches wide, for Unit 1.
- Six strips, 1½ inches wide, for Unit 4.
- Two strips, 2½ inches wide, for Unit 6.

FROM GREEN FABRIC, CUT:

- Six strips, 1½ inches wide, for Unit 3.
- Four strips, 1½ inches wide, for Unit 4.

FROM ORANGE-SPOTTED FABRIC, CUT:

- Two strips, 1½ inches wide, for Unit 3.
- One strip, 1½ inches wide, for Unit 6.

FROM PINK-AND-RED-PATTERNED FABRIC, CUT:

- Nine strips, 2½ inches wide, for the binding. Join the strips, end to end, using 45-degree seams, and press seams to one side.

FROM VARIOUS APPLIQUÉ FABRICS, TRACE AND CUT:

- 64 Circles, 14 Flowers, eight Trees, and four Corner Trees, using a gel pen or 2B pencil to trace the shapes. Fussy-cut (page 195) the shapes so that you have interesting patterns, leaving enough space between each to have ¼-inch seam allowance all around. Cut out the shapes using scissors and lay them flat in a heavy book to prevent creasing.

Constructing the quilt top

This quilt is based on an old block pattern called Burgoyne Surrounded. There are 12 blocks, laid out in four rows of three, separated by sashing strips. The separate units of the blocks are made first.

UNIT 1

Unit 1 has two different sets: 1A and 1B.

1 Take the two 1½-inch strips of crimson and two of the 1½-inch black fabric strips for Unit 1 and sew them together into two pairs along the long edge. Press the seam allowance toward the black fabric.

2 Trim the selvage off the ends of the paired strips and cross cut into 1½-inch segments, creating 48 pieces, 1½ x 2½ inches, with one crimson square and one black square.

3 Piece two cut strips together into a four-patch pair, reversing the crimson and black like a checkerboard (Diagram 1). Repeat to make 24 four-patch units, each 2½ inches square. This is Unit 1A. Set aside.

4 Repeat Steps 1–3 with two 1½-inch-wide orange print strips and the remaining two 1½-inch-wide black strips to make 24 of Unit 1B.

UNIT 2

5 From the eight black 2½-inch-wide strips for Unit 2, cross cut 96 rectangles, each 3½ x 2½ inches. This is Unit 2 (Diagram 2). Set aside.

UNIT 3

6 Take the two 1½-inch-wide strips of orange-spotted fabric for Unit 3 and sew them together into pairs with two of the 1½-inch-wide black strips, as for Unit 1, Step 1. From these strips, cross cut 48 rectangles, each 1½ x 2½ inches, as for Unit 1, Step 2.

7 Take the six 1½-inch-wide strips of green fabric for Unit 3 and sew them together into pairs with the six remaining 1½-inch-wide black strips, as for Unit 1, Step 1. From these strips, cross cut 96 squares, each 2½ inches.

8 Reversing the pieces to create a checkerboard effect, sew a 2½-inch square to either side of a 1½ x 2½-inch rectangle, creating a unit, 2½ x 5½ inches (Diagram 3). Repeat to make 48 pieces. This is Unit 3. Set aside.

Diagram 1
Unit 1

Unit 1A (make 24)   Unit 1B (make 24)

Diagram 2
Unit 2 (cut 96)

Diagram 3
Unit 3 (make 48)

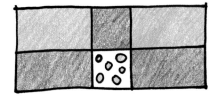

Diagram 4
Unit 4

4A (make 24)

4B (make 24)

4C (make 15)

4D (make 5)

Diagram 5
Unit 5 (cut 48)

Diagram 6
Unit 6 (make 12)

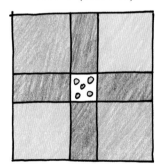

UNIT 4

Unit 4 has four different sets: 4A, 4B, 4C, and 4D.

9 Take the 14 black, six crimson, six orange-print, and four green 1½-inch strips for Unit 4 and sew them together along the length in the following color combinations:

  • Two sets (six strips total) of crimson, black, orange-print. From this set, cut 40 rectangles, each 1½ x 3½ inches.

  • Two sets of black, crimson, black. From this set, cut 39 rectangles, each 1½ x 3½ inches.

  • Two sets of black, orange-print, black. From this set, cut 29 rectangles, each 1½ x 3½ inches.

  • Two sets of crimson, black, green. From this set, cut 48 rectangles, each 1½ x 3½ inches.

  • Two sets of orange-print, black, green. From this set, cut 48 rectangles, each 1½ x 3½ inches.

  • Press all the seams toward the colored fabric.

10 Referring to Diagram 4, sew the pieces into nine-patch units to create 24 of Unit 4A and 24 of Unit 4B for the blocks, and 15 of Unit 4C and five of Unit 4D for the sashing. Set aside.

UNIT 5

11 From the seven black 3½-inch strips for Unit 5, cross cut 48 rectangles, each 3½ x 5½ inches. This is Unit 5 (Diagram 5). Set aside.

UNIT 6

12 Take the four black, two crimson, two orange-print, and one orange-spotted strips for Unit 6 and sew a crimson 2½-inch strip to one long edge of a black 1½-inch strip. Sew an orange-print 2½-inch strip to the remaining long edge of the black strip. Make two sets like this and press the seams toward the colored fabric. This is Set 1.

13 Sew a black 2½-inch strip to either side the 1½-inch orange-spotted strip. Press the seams towards the orange-spotted fabric. This is Set 2.

14 From the Set 1 strips, cross cut 24 rectangles, 2½ x 5½ inches.

15 From the Set 2 strip, cross cut 12 rectangles, each 1½ x 5½ inches.

16 Sew a Set 1 rectangle to either side of a Set 2 rectangle, taking care to alternate the colors (Diagram 6), creating a nine-patch unit. Press. Make 12 and set aside.

ASSEMBLING THE BLOCKS

The blocks are assembled in vertical strips. Refer to the Block Assembly Diagram to make sure you have the colored pieces running in the right direction. Lay the various components of the block out next to the sewing machine, making sure you have everything in the right place and ready to go.

17 For Strip 1, sew in the following order: Unit 1A, Unit 2, Unit 3, Unit 2, Unit 1B. (Make 12.)

18 For Strip 2, sew in the following order: Unit 2, Unit 4A, Unit 5, Unit 4B, Unit 2. (Make 12.)

19 For Strip 3, sew in the following order: Unit 3, Unit 5, Unit 6, Unit 5, Unit 3. (Make 12.)

20 For Strip 4, sew together in the following order: Unit 2, Unit 4B, Unit 5, Unit 4A, Unit 2. (Make 12.)

21 For Strip 5, sew in the following order: Unit 1B, Unit 2, Unit 3, Unit 2, Unit 1A. (Make 12.)

22 Next, sew all the strips together in order, from Row 1 to 5, taking care to match the seams to ensure neat points. The finished block should measure 15½ inches square. Press the twelve blocks carefully.

SASHING

23 Sew a 15½ x 3½-inch black sashing strip to the left-hand side of a block, and then continue alternating sashing strips and blocks, creating a row of three blocks, divided by sashing strips, starting and ending with a sashing strip (three blocks, four sashing strips). Repeat to make four rows like this.

24 Next, sew one of the remaining Unit 4 nine-patch units (4C and 4D) to the short end of a sashing strip, then continue alternating sashing strips and nine-patch units, creating a row of three sashing strips divided by nine-patch units, beginning and ending with a nine-patch unit (three sashing strips, four nine-patch units). Take care to look at the photograph of the quilt to see which direction the colors in the nine-patch units should run. Repeat to make five rows like this.

25 Starting with a sashing row, sew the sashing to the top of a block row, matching the seams. Repeat until you have sewn all the sashing and block rows together, alternating block and sashing rows, beginning and ending with a sashing row (four block rows, five sashing rows). Press the quilt top carefully. Measure the quilt top carefully through the center in both directions. It should now measure 57½ x 75½ inches.

Block Assembly Diagram

26 Trim two of the black border strips to measure 10½ x 75½ inches. Find the center of the border strip and the center of the left side of the quilt and pin. Match and pin the ends, and then pin the edges in between, easing if necessary. Sew. Repeat with the right-hand side of the quilt.

27 Trim remaining border strips to measure 10½ x 77½ inches. Repeat the above steps to attach the strips to the top and bottom of the quilt. Press.

APPLIQUÉ

Read the instructions for Appliqué on page 198 before proceeding.

28 With pins or appliqué glue, center the Circles on the sashing between the blocks, using the photograph as a guide to placement. Following the instructions for needle-turn appliqué on page 198, appliqué in place.

29 When you have completed all the circles, pin or glue the Corner Trees in place and appliqué.

30 Find the center of the border strips and use this measurement to place the Trees and Flowers in a pleasing spacing along each border. Pin or glue, then appliqué as before. You might find it easier to baste the Flowers to the background using a contrasting cotton thread, about ½ inch in from the edge. Finger-press around the edge of the Flower all along the pen line, then appliqué it in place, clipping carefully into the inside curves to help turn them under. Your quilt top is complete!

Backing, quilting, and binding

Cut the backing fabric crosswise in half, giving two 102-inch pieces. Remove the selvages and sew the lengths together to form one backing piece. Press the seam open.

Refer to pages 204–211 for instructions on finishing.

I hand-quilted Charlotte Sometimes by echo-quilting all the colored piecing and appliqué with gray perle cotton.

Shared Inspiration

~+~+~+~+~+~

Many quilt historians describe the Lone Star as the pinnacle of every quilter's career.

Lone Star patterns are on many quilters' lists of things to make "one day"!

That day is now, as we have each made a Lone Star quilt with quite different results.

Over the Border is a color story, madly contained and shimmering out of control at the same

time. Sunday is soft and Amish, with special circular star-pieced sections in the corners.

Keeping the fabrics simple gives this quilt a lovely, restful feeling.

Over the Border

Sunday

Over the Border

 Kathy Doughty

THE IDEA

Making a Lone Star quilt is a quilter's rite of passage. This was on the design wall longer than any other project in the book. I loved the warm and cool colors, joined by one of my stable of brown fabrics. But I was stuck on the border. Just when I was about to abandon it, a friend walked in with the yellow-and-brown-striped fabric. Problem solved! It always amazes us how a fabric can sit in the shop and then, suddenly, is the perfect choice. This is also a great stash quilt. The spotted fabric works well as a mid-tone neutral, setting off the brighter-colored fabrics in the star. Remember, when using a spotted fabric, that if they are all the same size, the effect is as a neutral. But if it appears too busy, it is easy to simply pick a solid background.

Finished quilt size

Queen, 90½ inches square

Materials and tools

2⅝ yards yellow-spotted fabric for background

1⅛ yards brown fabric for stars and center diamonds

A total of ⅞ yard cool-colored fabrics, at least 3 inches wide

A total of ⅞ yard warm-colored fabrics, at least 3 inches wide

2½ yards striped fabric (allowing for directional stripe) or 1⅞ yards for standard borders

⅔ yard fabric for binding

8½ yards backing fabric

97-inch-square wool batting

45-degree ruler for cutting diamonds (optional) or template plastic

2B pencil

Rotary cutter, quilter's ruler, and cutting mat

Neutral-colored cotton thread for piecing

NOTE: *It is recommended that all fabrics be 100 percent cotton, and be ironed. Requirements are based on fabric 44 inches wide. Unless otherwise stated, all seam allowances are ¼ inch throughout. Color test any dark fabrics that you are using (see page 189), and wash them before cutting if they run.*

Please read all instructions before starting.

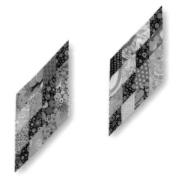

Templates

If you are not using the 45-degree ruler, trace the Template 1 diamond outline (on the pattern sheet) onto template plastic with a sharp 2B pencil. Cut out accurately using sharp scissors—not fabric scissors!

Cutting

All fabrics are strip cut across the width of the fabric from fold to selvage unless otherwise specified, or unless you are using a directional print (cut off all selvages first). Cut the largest pieces first.

FROM YELLOW-SPOTTED BACKGROUND FABRIC, CUT:

- Three strips, 12½ inches wide. Cross cut eight squares, each 12½ inches.
- Two strips, 10⅞ inches wide. Cross cut four squares, each 10⅞ inches. Cut these squares in half diagonally, giving eight half-square triangles for setting the Star Corners.
- Two strips, 3½ inches wide. Cross cut 32 squares, each 3½ inches, for the Star Corners.
- Two strips, 5½ inches wide. Cross cut eight squares, each 5½ inches. Cut these squares in half diagonally, and in half again, giving 32 quarter-square triangles, for the Star Corners.
- Four strips, 1¾ inches wide. These strips will be used as filler strips to make the inner section of the quilt big enough for the Star Corners.

FROM BROWN FABRIC, CUT:

- 13 strips, 2⅝ inches wide. Using a 45-degree ruler or Template 1, cross cut 128 diamond shapes.

FROM COOL-COLORED FABRICS, CUT:

- At least 10 strips, 2⅝ inches wide. Using a 45-degree ruler or Template 1, cross cut 96 diamond shapes in a variety of cool colors.

FROM WARM-COLORED FABRICS, CUT:

- At least 10 strips, 2⅝ inches wide. Using a 45-degree ruler or Template 1, cross cut 96 diamond shapes in a variety of warm colors.

FROM STRIPED BORDER FABRIC, CUT:

- Four strips, 10½ inches wide, along the length. Set aside for Inner Borders.

Or, if you are using a directional stripe, cut (in this order):

- Two strips, 10½ inches wide, across the width.
- Two strips, 10½ inches wide, along the length of the remaining fabric.
- Two strips, 10½ inches wide, across the width of the leftover fabric.

(Keeping the pattern correct, join one of these strips to one end of each of the crosswise strips that you cut first.)

FROM OUTER BORDER FABRIC, CUT:

- Nine strips, 5 inches wide. Sew them together, end to end, and set aside for mitered Outer Borders.

FROM BINDING FABRIC, CUT:

- Nine strips, 2½ inches wide. Join the strips, end to end, using 45-degree seams, and press seams to one side.

Constructing the quilt top

DIAMOND PANELS (MAKE 16)

1   Separate the diamonds into eight sets of 16 diamonds (12 warm colors plus four brown diamonds) and another eight sets of 16 diamonds (12 cool colors plus four brown diamonds)—16 sets in total.

2   Following Diagrams 1 and 2, sew these diamonds together in rows of four, taking special note of the placement of the brown diamond in each row. (The brown diamonds should be first, second, third, and fourth in the rows, respectively, to make them "move" through the middle.) Be sure to cut off all the ears as you go along.

3   Sew these rows of four together, matching the points, to make a diamond panel.

4   Repeat this process to make eight warm and eight cool diamond panels. Set four warm and four cool diamond panels aside for the outer ring.

CENTER STAR

5   Pinning all points, sew one warm diamond panel to one cool diamond panel. Repeat for the remaining six panels (four pairs in total).

6   Mark a point with a pencil ¼ inch in from all four corners on the yellow background squares. (We will use this point to inset a square between two diamond panels).

7   Starting in the middle, drop the needle into the marked dot and through the seam of the two joined diamond panels, ¼ inch in from the edge. Sew to the outer point. Go back to the middle and sew out to the remaining outer point (Diagram 3).

8   Repeat this process until you have sewn a square into each of the four pairs (Diagram 4, page 88).

9   Keeping the warm/cool color sequence correct and matching all points, sew these units together in pairs, and then sew the two halves together to form the center star.

10 Repeating Step 7, set in the remaining four background squares (Diagram 5, page 88).

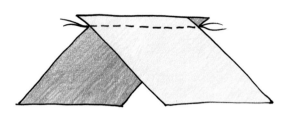

Diagram 1

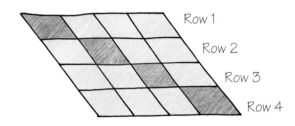

Diagram 2

Row 1
Row 2
Row 3
Row 4

Diagram 3

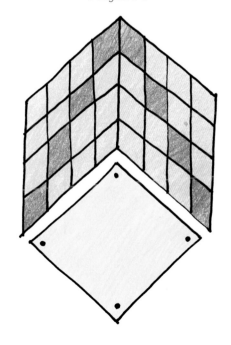

Diagram 4

Diagram 5

OUTER RING AND FILLER STRIPS

11 Matching the ¼-inch points on the background squares to the points of the reserved diamond panels for the outer ring, inset sew these panels in place (Diagram 6). Remember to keep the alternating warm/cool sequence.

12 With excess fabric extending beyond each edge, pin and sew the filler strips to the top, bottom, and two side edges. Use the ruler to trim the ends on an angle, even with the diamond panel's raw edge (Diagram 6).

STAR CORNERS (MAKE 8)

13 Make eight piles of eight brown diamonds, four 3½-inch corner squares, and four quarter-square triangles, for the Star Corners.

14 Mark all ¼-inch seam points on the wrong side of the squares and triangles with a pencil and a ruler for a better piecing result.

15 Start by sewing four pairs of brown diamonds together, then sew the pairs together into two half-stars, sewing only to ¼ inch from the edge that will have the background square or triangle set into it.

16 Sew the half-stars together to complete the star, again remembering to leave ¼ inch unstitched at each outer end of the seam.

17 Following Step 7 on page 87, set in the yellow corner square, starting at the inner corner, and sewing to the outer points. Repeat for each of the corner squares.

18 Matching the points, set in the quarter-square triangles, stitching from the apex out to the edge to complete the star (Diagram 7).

Diagram 6

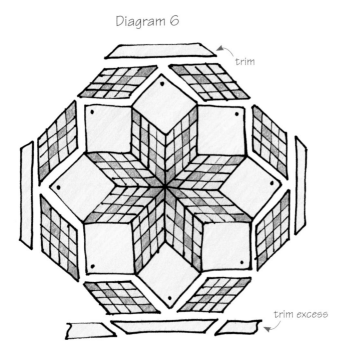

trim

trim excess

Diagram 7

19 Make eight Star Corners in this manner and set four aside for the Inner Border corners.

20 Match the straight sides of the half-square triangles to two adjacent sides of a Star Corner unit. Pin, and then sew them to form a large triangle (Diagram 8). Make four.

21 Match the inner point of the Star Corner to the middle of the two diamond panels in the outer ring, pin, and then sew in place. Repeat for the remaining three corners.

Diagram 8

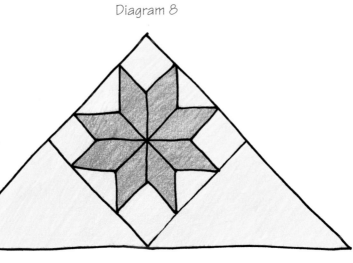

INNER BORDER

22 Measure the quilt top through the center in both directions. It should measure 61½ inches square. (If your measurements differ, you will need to adjust the Inner Borders accordingly.) Trim the four 10½-inch Inner Border strips to 61½ inches long. Pin the centers and ends, and then sew the top and bottom borders in place.

23 Sew two reserved Star Corners to each end of the remaining border strips, pin, and then sew the side borders in place.

OUTER BORDER

24 Measure the quilt top through the center in both directions. It should measure 81½ inches square. (If your measurements differ, you will need to adjust the Outer Borders accordingly.) The outer borders are mitered, which means that the border length needs to allow for the corner. From the joined Outer Border strip, cut four strips, each 5 x 92 inches (or add 10½ inches to your quilt top measurement to obtain the length of your Outer Borders.)

25 Referring to the instructions for Adding Borders on page 203, attach the mitered borders to the quilt top. Your quilt top is complete!

Backing, quilting, and binding

Cut the backing fabric crosswise into three 102-inch pieces. Remove the selvages and stitch the pieces together up the middle seams. Press the seam allowance open and press the backing piece carefully.

Refer to pages 204–211 for instructions on finishing.

Over the Border is machine-quilted with off-white cotton in a pattern called Swirl & Twirl, with a 6-inch repeat.

Sunday

 Sarah Fielke

THE IDEA

I named this quilt Sunday because it weaved its quiet way through many Sundays at my house while I hand-quilted it. As it is a large project, the quilting took a long time, but I enjoyed every stitch; watching the plain fabrics take on their own texture was a little bit of quilting magic.

This quilt was inspired, again, by an antique quilt. There is no way of knowing the size of the original, but even the drafting of the project was exciting as I saw that it would look just how I imagined.

Lone Star quilts are not easy. They require very exact piecing and careful cutting to avoid puckering and buckling at the center! Take your time, check and re-check, and let the rhythm of a project this size be its own reward.

Finished quilt size

Queen, 95 inches square

Materials and tools

4¾ yards chocolate-brown fabric for background

1⅝ yards red fabric for star

1⅝ yards yellow fabric for star

2⅛ yards pink fabric for star

1⅛ yards green fabric for star

1⅝ yards blue fabric for star

8½ yards backing fabric

102-inch-square cotton batting

2B pencil

Chalk pencil

Quarter-inch ruler

Template plastic or a large sheet of paper

Rotary cutter, quilter's ruler, and cutting mat

Creative Grids Turn-A-Round Diamond Ruler (optional)

Neutral-colored cotton thread for piecing

Cotton thread to match appliqué fabrics

Appliqué needles

Appliqué glue

6 balls dark brown perle cotton no. 8 for quilting

NOTE: *It is recommended that all fabrics be 100 percent cotton, and be ironed. Requirements are based on fabric 44 inches wide. Unless otherwise stated, all seam allowances are ¼ inch throughout. Color test any dark fabrics that you are using (see page 189), and wash them before cutting if they run.*

Please read all instructions before starting.

Templates

The templates are on the pattern sheet. Trace the quarter-circle outline onto template plastic or paper, using a sharp 2B pencil. If you are not using the Diamond Ruler, you also need to trace the Diamond outline onto template plastic or paper. Cut out both shapes accurately using sharp scissors—not fabric scissors!

Cutting

All fabrics are strip cut across the width of the fabric from fold to selvage unless otherwise specified (cut off all selvages first). Cut the largest pieces first. The 392 diamonds for the Center Star and 48 for the Outer Stars are all cut in the same manner. You can use either the Turn-A-Round Diamond Ruler with a 4-inch diamond size, your traced plastic template, or the 45-degree line on your straight quilter's ruler (use the paper template under the ruler as a guide) to cut diamonds with a side length of 4¾ inches.

FROM RED FABRIC, CUT:

- Nine strips, 3⅜ inches wide. Cross cut 72 diamonds for the Center Star.
- Three strips, 6½ inches wide. Cross cut into 16 squares, each 6½ inches, for the Outer Star backgrounds.
- Three strips, 2½ inches wide. Put these strips aside for binding.

FROM GREEN FABRIC, CUT:

- Nine strips, 3⅜ inches wide. Cross cut 72 diamonds for the Center Star.
- Three strips, 2½ inches wide. Put these strips aside for binding.

FROM YELLOW FABRIC, CUT:

- 11 strips, 3⅜ inches wide. Cross cut 88 diamonds for the Center Star.
- Four strips, 3⅜ inches wide. Cross cut 32 diamonds for the Outer Stars.
- Three strips, 2½ inches wide. Put these strips aside for binding.

FROM PINK FABRIC, CUT:

- Eight strips, 3⅜ inches wide. Cross cut 64 diamonds for the Center Star.
- Six strips, 6½ inches wide. Cross cut into 32 squares, each 6½ inches, for the Outer Star backgrounds.
- Three strips, 2½ inches wide. Put these strips aside for binding.

FROM BLUE FABRIC, CUT:

- 12 strips, 3⅜ inches. Cross cut 96 diamonds for the Center Star.
- Two strips, 3⅜ inches wide. Cross cut 16 diamonds for the Outer Stars.
- Three strips, 2½ inches wide. Put these strips aside for binding.

FROM CHOCOLATE-BROWN FABRIC, CUT:

- Four squares, each 28 inches.
- One square, 30 inches. Cross cut this square twice on the diagonal to make four quarter-square triangles. Do not cut these until you are ready to piece them, as that is a lot of bias to stretch!
- Six strips, 1½ inches wide. Cross cut into 48 strips, each 1½ x 6 inches, for the Outer Star borders.
- Six strips, 1½ inches wide. Cross cut into 48 strips, each 1½ x 7 inches, for the Outer Star borders.

Constructing the quilt top

CENTER STAR

Accuracy is very important when piecing a Lone Star quilt. If you have not worked with diamonds before or have not inset-pieced before, we recommend you mark the ¼-inch seams with a pencil onto the back of each diamond before piecing. This will help you to line the diamonds up correctly for sewing and see where to start and stop sewing some seams.

Because you are dealing with lots of pieces, it is very helpful to lay out each whole diamond in sequence before you sew the small diamonds into rows and the rows into the larger pieced diamond. Being able to visualize the diamond as you work will make the star assembly instructions read more clearly, and you will quickly spot any mistake in the sequence.

The Center Star is made up of eight diamond-shaped panels of 49 diamonds each (seven rows of seven diamonds).

1 For each panel, piece the diamonds into strips as follows (Diagram 1):

Row 1	Row 2	Row 3	Row 4	Row 5	Row 6	Row 7
red	green	yellow	pink	red	blue	green
green	yellow	pink	red	blue	green	yellow
yellow	pink	red	blue	green	yellow	blue
pink	red	blue	green	yellow	blue	pink
red	blue	green	yellow	blue	pink	red
blue	green	yellow	blue	pink	red	yellow
green	yellow	blue	pink	red	yellow	blue

2 Press the seams to one side and trim the tips off the diamonds.

3 Continue in this way until you have seven strips, working through each of the fabrics you have cut. Pay close attention to the order in which you are sewing the diamonds together, and keep to the sequence.

4 When you have your seven rows assembled, sew the strips together in order (following Diagram 1), taking care to match your seams and to keep the strips in order of color. Do not forget that you are sewing a diamond, so the strips have to be staggered. Sew all seven strips

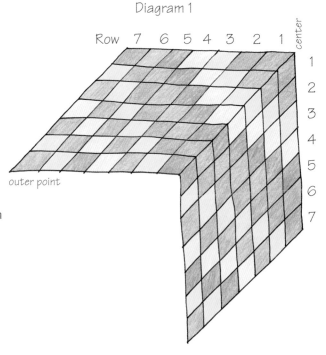

Diagram 1

Row 7 6 5 4 3 2 1 center

outer point

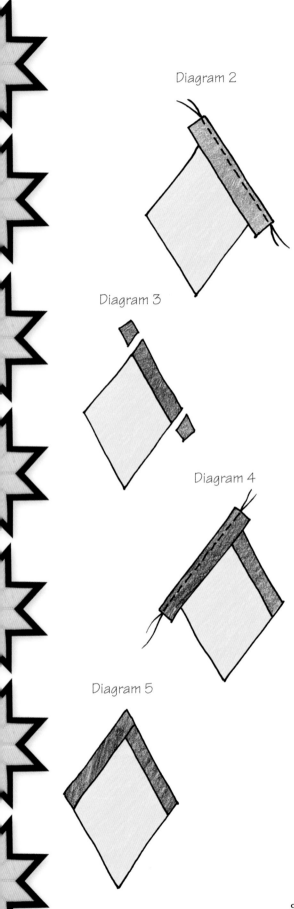

Diagram 2

Diagram 3

Diagram 4

Diagram 5

together to make a large diamond unit. Press carefully. Repeat until you have assembled all eight diamond units.

ASSEMBLING CENTER STAR

5 Being very careful to match your seams, sew together two diamond units into a pair. (The red diamonds should form a "v" at the center seam of each panel.) Stop sewing ¼ inch from the outer edge of the panels, at the corner where the backgrounds will be inserted. This will enable more accurate and easier piecing of the inset seam here later. Repeat this step until you have four pairs of diamonds.

6 Taking care to keep the color sequence correct, stitch two diamond pairs together to form half the star, stopping sewing ¼ inch from the edge as before. Repeat for the second half of the star.

7 Carefully matching and pinning seams, sew the two halves together across the center seam. Carefully press your star open and admire!

OUTER STARS

The Outer Stars are assembled in much the same way as the Center Star—just easier! You need to make four complete stars and four half-stars.

8 Take eight of the yellow diamonds for the Outer Stars. Sew a 6 x 1½-inch chocolate-brown strip along the left-hand edge of the diamond (Diagram 2). Using the diamond ruler or template as a guide, trim the edges even with the yellow diamond (Diagram 3).

9 Sew a 7-inch strip to the right-hand side of the diamond (Diagram 4) and trim as before (Diagram 5). Repeat with remaining seven diamonds.

10 Sew the diamonds into four pairs, and then sew the pairs together into two half-stars (Diagram 6). Remember to sew only to ¼ inch from the edge that will have the background square set into it.

11 Sew the half-stars together to complete the star, again remembering to leave ¼ inch unstitched at each outer end of the seam.

12 Repeat Steps 8 to 10 and Step 11 as appropriate, to make four yellow complete stars and four blue half-stars.

OUTER STAR BACKGROUNDS

13 If you haven't already done so, mark with dots exactly ¼ inch in at the corner of the pink and red 6½-inch background squares and the inset edges of the stars and half-stars.

14 Starting with the full stars, carefully pin a pink 6½-inch square along the edge of one star point from the center dots out, right sides together.

NOTE: *The squares are too big for the star points! This is to allow for the stars to be trimmed into circles for appliqué, and you will need the extra fabric.*

15 Begin by putting your needle down through the dots you have drawn at the corner of the square. Using an exact ¼-inch seam, sew along the edge from the center out. Return to the center and pin the other edge of the square to the other side of the star. Repeat until you have inserted all eight squares around the star. Press the seams toward the star. Make four full stars in this manner.

16 Repeat the process for the four half-stars, using the red 6½-inch squares, and noting that one red square is cut in half diagonally for the lower edge of each half-star.

APPLIQUÉ

17 Fold a half-star in half and place the quarter-circle template on top of the star. Trace around the template with a chalk pencil or something similar, and then cut away the extra fabric, cutting ¼ inch outside the traced line (Diagram 7).

18 Take a large chocolate-brown quarter-square triangle and fold it in half. Finger-press a crease into the triangle. Center the half-star onto the triangle and glue in place with appliqué glue. Turn under ¼ inch on the edge and carefully appliqué in place (see page 198), using thread to match the red background.

19 Repeat this process to appliqué a half-star to all four of the quarter-square triangles.

20 Prepare the four complete stars in the same way, folding them into quarters to trace the circle outline (Diagram 8). If you wish, you can make a complete circle or half-circle template, but you'll need a very large sheet of paper! To center the circles for appliqué, fold the large corner squares into quarters, and then proceed with the appliqué as before. Make four corner squares.

21 To avoid show-through, carefully trim the brown fabric away from behind all the appliquéd panels, cutting ¼ inch from the stitching.

QUILT BODY ASSEMBLY

22 Mark with dots exactly ¼ inch in at the corner of the large squares, the quarter-square triangles, and the diamond panels of the Center Star.

23 Beginning with your large chocolate-brown squares, carefully pin the square along the edge of one Center Star star point from the center dots out, right sides together.

NOTE: *Once again, the squares and triangles are too big for the star points. This is to allow for everyone's varying ¼-inch seams and to allow you to trim the quilt back to be square after piecing in these edges.*

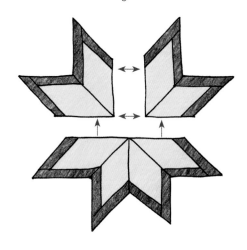

Diagram 6

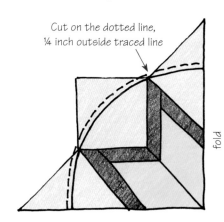

Diagram 7

Cut on the dotted line,
¼ inch outside traced line

fold

Diagram 8

24 Begin by putting your needle down through the dot you have drawn at the corner of the square. Using an exact ¼-inch seam, sew along the edge from the center out. Return to the center and pin the other edge of the square to the other side of the star.

25 Repeat this process for all four corners of the quilt and the center quarter-square triangles. Carefully press all the seams toward the diamond panels.

26 Trim the excess fabric back so that the edges of the quilt are square. Your quilt top is complete!

Backing, quilting, and binding

Cut the backing fabric crosswise into three pieces, each 102 inches long. Remove the selvages and sew the lengths together to form one backing piece. Press the seams open.

Refer to pages 204–211 for instructions on finishing.

I hand-quilted Sunday by outline-quilting each diamond approximately ⅛ inch from the seam, all the way around. I quilted the chocolate-brown background in a diamond grid using the seams from the star as a guide. For the binding, from your reserved 2½-inch strips of colored star fabrics, cut a number of strips of varying lengths. Join the strips, end to end, alternating the colors, and using 45-degree seams, until you have a strip about 11¾ yards long. Press seams to one side. Proceed with binding as usual (see Binding on page 210).

Shared Inspiration

❧❧❧

We all have a growing stash of fabric and fabric bits. We can't justify the next purchase if we aren't using something precious we have collected before. It is also nearly impossible for any one of us to toss out a precious scrap of our favorite fabric, no matter how many times we have used it in quilts before. These two quilts use bits and pieces to create eye-catching mirages of carefully chosen fabrics. Don't tell anyone that they are nearly all scraps and they won't ever guess!

Stashbuster

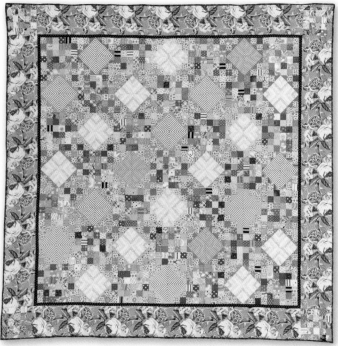

Coming Up Roses

Stashbuster

 Kathy Doughty

THE IDEA

Working in a fabric shop means I hear a lot of quilters say, "I have so much fabric already, I don't know what to do with it all!" In an effort to help out here, I made it my mission to make a quilt from my stash. Sometimes to do this, we need a bit of something extra which, in this case, was the white fabric.

I then did the separation of the fabrics into warm and cool colors and picked up one of my favorite rulers, the Marti Michell Kaleido-Ruler. Sewing all the strips together takes a bit of time, but adds so much to the quilt.

Finished quilt size

Throw or cot size, 47½ x 57½ inches
Block size: 10½ inches, including seam allowance

Materials and tools

1 yard white quilter's muslin
6 inches each of seven different spotted fabrics
Approximately 2¼ yards in total of fabric strips in a range of
    light/dark, warm/cool, small/large print, and so on, for stripped fabric
    (see Preparation, page 104)
⅝ yard spotted binding fabric
2⅞ yards backing fabric
55 x 65 inches cotton batting
Rotary cutter, quilter's ruler, and cutting mat
Marti Michell Large Kaleido-Ruler (optional, but recommended
    for accuracy)
Template plastic
2B pencil
Neutral-colored cotton thread for piecing
4 balls perle cotton no. 8 in colors to match or contrast with the fabrics,
    for quilting

NOTE: *It is recommended that all fabrics be 100 percent cotton, and be ironed. Requirements are based on fabric 44 inches wide. Unless otherwise stated, all seam allowances are ¼ inch throughout. Color test any dark fabrics that you are using (see page 189), and wash them before cutting if they run.*
    Please read all instructions before starting.

Diagram 1

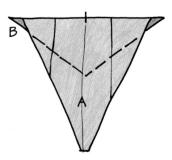

Diagram 2

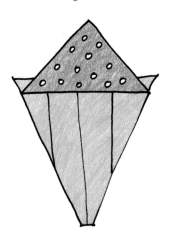

Diagram 3

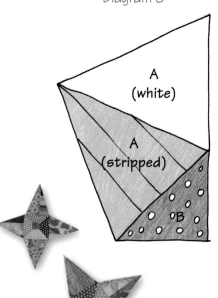

Templates

Templates A, B, and C are on the pattern sheet. If you are using templates instead of a ruler, trace Template A and Template B onto template plastic with a 2B pencil. Both cutting methods require a Template C Circle, so trace this too. Cut them out using sharp scissors—not fabric scissors!

Preparation

For the strip triangles and pieced borders, assemble your scraps and cut them into long lengths, ranging in width from 1½ to 3 inches. Sew them together along the length. Be sure to add contrast by alternating the size of the graphic patterns on the fabric, by warm or cool colors, or by light and dark. The more contrast you can work into your strips, the more exciting the results will be. For the triangles, cut the sewn strips into 5½-inch lengths across the strips and sew them together, end to end, until there are enough for six long pieced strips, each 5½ x 42 inches. For the pieced borders, cut the sewn strips into 4-inch lengths across the strips and sew them together, end to end, until you have about 200 inches.

TIP: *Store cool-color strips and warm-color strips separately. That way, it will be easy to alternate colors when assembling the strips.*

Cutting

All fabrics are cut across the width of the fabric from fold to selvage (cut off all selvages first). When starting a new project, make one complete block first, to ensure all measurements are right before cutting all the fabric.

FROM QUILTER'S MUSLIN, CUT:
- Six strips, 5½ inches wide. Using the Kaleido-Ruler or Template A, cross cut triangles from each strip to give 80 triangles in all (20 blocks with four white triangles in each).

FROM MULTICOLORED PIECED FABRIC, CUT:
- Six strips, 5½ x 42 inches. Using the Kaleido-Ruler or Template A, cross cut triangles from each strip to give 80 triangles in all (20 blocks with four stripped triangles in each).
- From the 4-inch-wide pieced strip, you will need two strips, each 4 x 50½ inches, and two strips, each 4 x 47½ inches, for the borders. (Do not cut borders exactly until you have constructed the quilt top.)

FROM SEVEN ASSORTED SPOTTED FABRICS, CUT:

- One strip, 3¾ inches wide, from each color (seven strips in all).
  Using the sharp angle corner of the ruler or Template B, cross cut
  80 half-square triangles in a variety of colors.
- 20 circles, using Template C, for the yo-yos (also called Suffolk puffs).

FROM SPOTTED BINDING FABRIC, CUT:

- Five strips, 2½ inches wide. Join the strips, end to end, using
  45-degree seams, and press seams to one side.

Constructing the quilt top

TIP: *Before sewing, stand back and view the placement of
the blocks, being mindful of color and texture balance. It is
also helpful to look through the lens of a camera to get a more
concentrated view of the layout. If using striped fabric, check that
the stripes are going in the intended direction. Rearrange the
blocks until they are all balanced throughout the quilt.*

KALEIDOSCOPE BLOCKS (MAKE 20)

1 Start with the colorful stripped triangles. With right sides together,
   position a spotted corner half-square triangle beneath the base of the
   larger stripped triangle so that the tips of the smaller triangle are equally
   visible on either side (Diagram 1). For positioning, it is helpful to finger-
   press the middle of each piece, match the middles, and then sew along
   the base of the triangles. Strip piece all 80 triangles of each size together
   in this manner. Press seam toward the corner triangle (Diagram 2).

2 With right sides together, position a white triangle over a stripped
   triangle and sew from the apex to the base. Press seam away from the
   Template B corner, regardless of the colors. This unit is one quarter
   of a block (Diagram 3).

3 Sew these units into pairs, starting ¼ inch away from the apex at the
   seam line and being careful not to sew down the seam allowance.
   By doing this, the fabrics at the point will lie flat when finished. Each
   stitched pair constitutes half a block (Diagram 4).

4 To complete the block, sew the halves together from the outside seam
   to the center, and from the opposite outside seam to the center
   (Diagram 5). Press all seam allowances clockwise.

ASSEMBLING THE BLOCKS

5 Assemble and sew the blocks in four rows of five blocks, carefully
   matching all points and corners in the blocks. Measure the top through
   the center in both directions. It should now measure 40½ x 50½ inches.
   If your measurements differ, adjust your border measurements.

Diagram 4

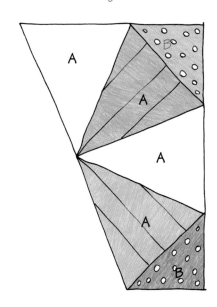

Diagram 5

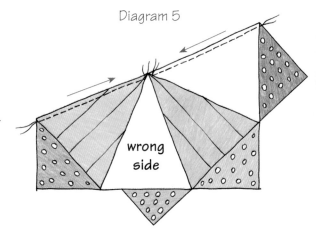

wrong
side

6 From the pieced border fabric, cut two strips, 4 x 50½ inches, for side borders, and two strips, 4 x 47½ inches, for top and bottom borders.

7 To add the borders, fold the quilt top and the border strips in half and mark the center points. Starting with the side borders, match the center of the border to the center of the quilt top and pin in place. Then match and pin the rest of the border in place as well. Sew border to quilt top and repeat on the other side.

8 Add the top and bottom borders. Your quilt top is complete!

Backing, quilting, and binding

Cut the backing fabric crosswise in half. Remove the selvages and stitch the pieces together up the middle seam. Press the seam allowance open and press the backing piece carefully.

Refer to pages 204–211 for instructions on finishing.

Stashbuster was hand-quilted with perle cotton in colors to match or contrast with the fabrics. The quilt has red lines running through the white spaces to connect them to the bright colors of the pieced sections and to create a secondary square pattern. The corner squares are echo-quilted around the seams of the triangles. The yo-yos are added after quilting.

Yo-yos

With the wrong side of the fabric circle facing you, work a row of running stitches around the edge, turning under ¼ inch, and concealing the knot within the seam allowance (Diagram 6). At the starting point, pull up the thread to gather the stitches tightly into the center, take the needle through the center hole to the back, and secure with a knot. Make 20 yo-yos in this way, and then slipstitch the yo-yos in place over the points in the center of the blocks and at the corners, using sewing thread that matches the yo-yo.

Diagram 6

Coming Up Roses

 Sarah Fielke

THE IDEA

Everything's coming up roses when you make this quilt. Easy pieced blocks use up tons of scrap fabrics, so all you have to do is find a beautiful border and some coordinating stripes.

This quilt is a great exercise in controlling a scrap project. You can put any scraps you please into the 36-patch blocks, but the stripes, triangles, and blue squares in the second block and the floral border hold everything together and make order from chaos.

When I started this quilt, it was just going to be a quickie, to try to stem the tide of my overflowing scrap bins! As I sewed, the blocks just seemed to multiply, and before long it was a single bed, a double, a king . . . and still my scrap bin overflows. Maybe I'll have to make another one.

Finished quilt size

King bed, 112 inches square
Block size: 12½ inches, including seam allowance

Materials and tools

⅓ yard each of 16 fabrics, or scrap totalling 5¼ yards
⅞ yard multi-striped fabric (more if fussy-cutting: see Cutting, page 110)
¼ yard each blue-, orange-, green-, and pink-striped fabric (more if fussy-cutting)
1½ yards blue-floral-spotted accent fabric for blocks
⅛ yard each of 12 pink fabrics, or pink scraps totalling 1½ yards
⅜ yard red-and-green-spotted fabric for Inner Border
2¾ yards rose border fabric
1 yard brown-spotted fabric for binding
10 yards backing fabric
118-inch-square cotton batting
Rotary cutter, quilter's ruler, and cutting mat
Neutral-colored cotton thread for piecing

NOTE: *It is recommended that all fabrics be 100 percent cotton, and be ironed. Requirements are based on fabric 44 inches wide. Unless otherwise stated, all seam allowances are ¼ inch throughout. Color test any dark fabrics that you are using (see page 189), and wash them before cutting if they run.*

Please read all instructions before starting.

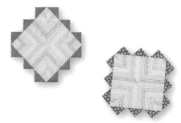

Cutting

All fabrics are strip cut across the width of the fabric from fold to selvage unless otherwise specified or unless you are using a directional print (cut off all selvages first). Cut the largest pieces first.

FROM 16 MIXED FABRICS OR SCRAP, CUT:

- Four strips, 2½ inches wide, from each fabric. Cross cut into 68 squares, each 2½ inches. Repeat with all 16 fabrics until you have a total of 968 squares. If you are using scrap fabrics, cut a total of 968 squares, each 2½ inches. (You will only use 956 squares, but cutting extra gives you a good range of scraps.)

FROM BLUE-FLORAL-SPOTTED FABRIC, CUT:

- 19 strips, 2½ inches wide. Cross cut into 292 squares, each 2½ inches.

CUTTING THE STRIPED FABRICS

When cutting the striped fabric, the fabric requirement given is based on cutting a half-square triangle, not a quarter-square. This means that the stripes will not run into the center, as in the original quilt; it will make a pattern that looks like the square has been folded. This is because this is actually the correct way to place the bias of your triangle. The effect is very nice, but different from the original.

If you want to cut the stripes as in the original quilt, please be very aware that this will put the bias of your triangles in the wrong place and you will have to be extra careful when cutting and piecing. Instructions are given for both versions, but you may need more fabric than specified if you are using a wide stripe or one with an unusual pattern.

To cut as for the original, cut your strip of fabric 4¾ inches and use the 45-degree line on your straight ruler to cut the triangles as illustrated in Diagram 1. You will get seven triangles from a strip, so you would need two strips for three blocks (four triangles per block). Otherwise:

Diagram 1

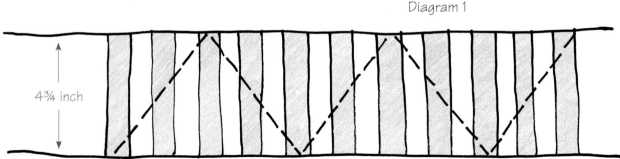

4¾ inch

FROM THE MULTI-STRIPED FABRIC, CUT:

- Four strips, 6⅞ inches wide. Cross cut into 24 squares, each 6⅞ inches. Cross cut these squares to yield 48 half-square triangles.

FROM EACH OF BLUE-, GREEN-, ORANGE-, AND PINK-STRIPED FABRICS, CUT:

- One strip, 6⅞ inches wide. Cross cut into six squares, each 6⅞ inches. Cross cut these squares to yield 12 half-square triangles from each fabric (48 triangles in total).

FROM EACH OF 12 PINK FABRICS, CUT:

- One strip, 2⅞ inches wide. Cross cut to yield 12 squares, each 2⅞ inches. Cross cut these squares to yield 24 half-square triangles from each fabric (288 half-square triangles in total; two sets of 12 triangles from each fabric).

FROM RED-AND-GREEN-SPOTTED FABRIC, CUT:

- Eight strips, 1½ inches wide, for the Inner Border.

FROM ROSE BORDER FABRIC, CUT:

- Five strips, 2½ inches wide. Cross cut into 50 squares, each 2½ inches, for the border corners.
- From the remaining fabric, cut eight strips, 10½ inches wide, for the Outer Border.

FROM BROWN-SPOTTED FABRIC, CUT:

- 13 strips, 2½ inches wide, for the binding. Join the strips, end to end, using 45-degree seams, and press seams to one side.

Constructing the quilt top

BLOCK 1

1. Sew the 2½-inch squares into rows of six squares, mixing and alternating the fabrics well as you go. The top and bottom row of each block (Rows 1 and 6) should begin and end with a 2½-inch square of blue-floral-spotted fabric. Therefore, you will need a total of 50 rows beginning and ending with a blue-floral-spotted square, and a total of 100 rows with six mixed squares.

2. Sew the rows together in blocks of six rows to make a 36-patch block. Rows 1 and 6 begin and end with a blue-floral-spotted square (Diagram 2). Continue until you have made 25 of Block 1. The finished block should measure 12½ inches square, including seam allowance. Press.

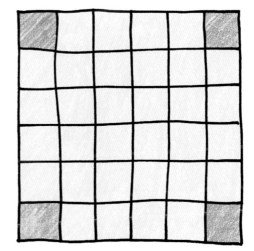

Diagram 2

Diagram 3

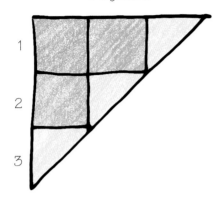

Diagram 4

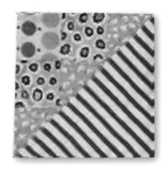

Diagram 5
Half-square triangles

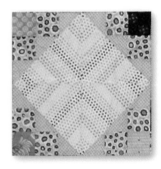

Diagram 6
Fussy-cut triangles

BLOCK 2

3 This block is assembled in quarters. For one quarter, first sew a 2½-inch square to a blue-floral-spotted 2½-inch square. Sew a pink triangle to the blue-floral-spotted square. This is Row 1.

4 Next, sew another identical pink triangle to a blue-floral-spotted square. This is Row 2. Referring to the diagram, sew Row 1 to Row 2, and then sew another identical pink triangle to the bottom to form a large triangle (Diagram 3).

5 Sew a striped triangle to this unit (Diagram 4). This is a quarter of the block. Repeat until you have four quarters of the block pieced, as per the diagram.

6 Sew two quarters into a pair and repeat with the remaining two quarters. Piece the halves together and press. This is Block 2. (Diagrams 5 and 6 show the difference between the fussy-cut and half-square striped triangles. If using the fussy-cut triangles, take great care not to stretch the bias edges as you stitch.)

7 Using the striped fabrics you have cut, make three green, three pink, three blue, and three orange blocks from the colored stripes, and 12 blocks from the multi-striped fabric, for a total of 24 of Block 2. The finished blocks should measure 12½ inches square, including seam allowance.

ASSEMBLING THE BLOCKS

8 Referring to the photograph for placement, lay the blocks in order on the floor or on a design wall. If you find that you would rather have the colors placed in a different way than on the original quilt, move them around until you are happy with the layout.

9 Sew the blocks into seven rows of seven blocks. The first block in Row 1 is Block 1, and the first block of Row 2 is Block 2. Alternating the blocks across and down the quilt, piece the seven rows together.

10 Press the seams carefully, and then sew the seven pieced rows together.

11 Measure the quilt top through the center in both directions. It should now measure 84½ inches square. If it does not, adjust your borders.

INNER BORDER

12 Take the 1½-inch-wide red-and-green-spotted strips and remove the selvages. Join the strips together into pairs, end to end, so that you have four long strips. Press.

13 Cut two of the long strips to measure 84½ inches exactly. Find the center of the sides of the quilt top and the center of the strip, and pin together. Match and pin the ends, and then pin the edges in between. This will prevent the borders from rippling when they are attached. Sew, and then repeat with the other side.

14 Trim both the remaining border strips to 86½ inches. Pin and sew, as described above, to the top and bottom of the quilt. Press.

OUTER BORDER

15 Measure your quilt through the center in both directions again. It should measure 86½ inches square. If it does not, you will need to adjust the length of your Outer Border strips.

16 Take two strips of the 10½-inch rose border fabric, remove the selvages, and sew together, end to end, to form one long strip. Trim the strip to measure 86½ inches. Repeat with the remaining strips until you have four border strips, each 10½ x 86½ inches.

17 Find the center of one side of the quilt top and the center of one of the Outer Border strips. Pin the centers together, match and pin the ends, and then pin the edges in between. Sew, and then repeat with another border strip on the opposite side of the quilt top. Press.

18 Take 50 of the remaining 2½-inch scrap squares and the 50 rose border 2½-inch squares, and piece four 25-patch corner blocks (five rows of five squares each), alternating the 2½-inch squares of border fabric with the scrap squares to form a checkerboard. Press.

19 Sew one corner block to each end of the remaining Outer Border strips. Matching centers and ends, as before, sew the remaining Outer Borders to the quilt top and press. Your quilt top is complete!

Backing, quilting, and binding

Cut the backing fabric crosswise into three pieces, each 120 inches long. Remove the selvages and sew the lengths together to form one backing piece. Press the seams open.

Refer to pages 204–211 for instructions on finishing.

I machine-quilted Coming Up Roses, as there is so much going on that I figured hand-quilting would disappear! The quilter created large roses in a neutral cream thread to work with the roses in the border.

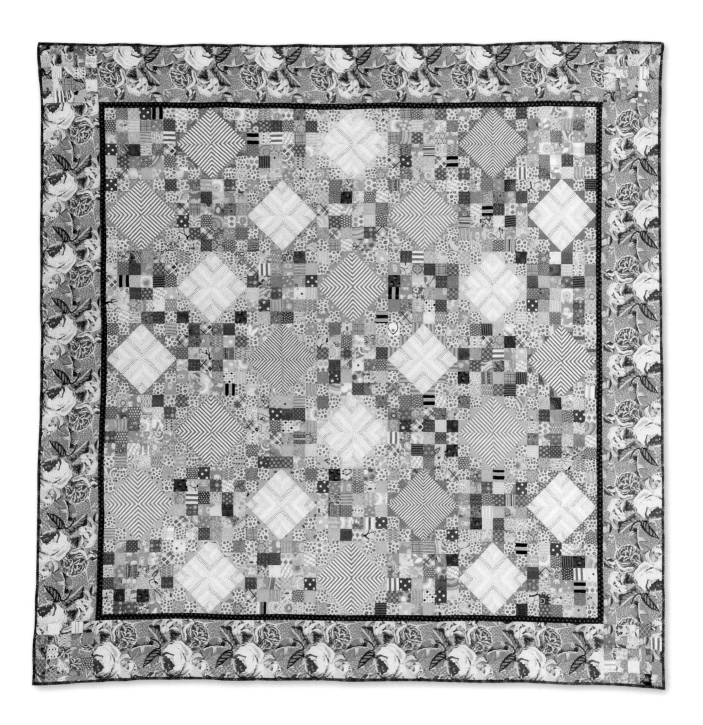

Shared Inspiration

✦✦✦✦✦

Spiderweb quilts are a fascinating use of color and design. They are also a fantastic way to weave scrap fabrics into a delightful quilt full of surprises and intrigue. Pop Stars is foundation-pieced onto calico or quilter's muslin, and uses a whole piece of fabric to make the stars at the center "pop" from the surface. Maple Leaf Rag is a similar pattern, but with a crazy-pieced central star, creating a focus on the web.

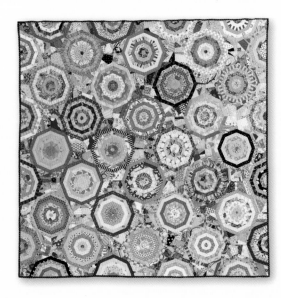

Maple Leaf Rag

Pop Stars

Pop Stars

Kathy Doughty

THE IDEA

I always quilt to music, often piecing bits of the song into the quilt as I go along. Like a favorite song, a stash quilt is warmly satisfying on several levels. The remnants of past projects have a bit of symmetry, made all the better by the idea of recycling what we love into a whole new tune.

The trick to a stash quilt is organizing the scraps. Separate fabrics into two piles: warm or cool, including all values, from light to dark. Select an inspiration fabric (or several that have the same impact) for the stars. Refer to your star fabric as you work through the strips, alternating from one pile to the other throughout, and organize your blocks so that you keep the same-value strips for the outside circle to make the spiderweb really work for you.

Finished quilt size

Queen, 83½ inches square
Block size: 21½ inches, including seam allowance

Materials and tools

4⅞ yards calico or quilter's muslin (56 inches wide) for foundation-piecing

3⅓ yards in total of a variety of solid fabrics for stars (this should be a minimum of 12 inches each of at least 10 fabrics, or proportionately more if using fewer fabrics)

7⅔ yards of a variety of scrap strips, each 1½ inches wide

⅝ yard binding fabric

5 yards backing fabric

95 x 98 inches cotton batting

Rotary cutter, quilter's ruler, and cutting mat

Template plastic (optional)

Kite-shaped ruler (optional, but recommended for accuracy)

3–5 balls perle cotton no. 8 in colors to match scraps, for quilting

NOTE: *It is recommended that all fabrics be 100 percent cotton, and be ironed. Requirements are based on fabric 44 inches wide. Unless otherwise stated, all seam allowances are ¼ inch throughout. Color test any dark fabrics that you are using (see page 189), and wash them before cutting if they run.*

Please read all instructions before starting.

Templates

Templates A, B, and C are on the pattern sheet. If you are not using the triangle ruler, trace Template A (full shape), B/BR (half shape), and C (triangle point) onto template plastic using a 2B pencil, and cut out accurately with sharp scissors—not fabric scissors! Label your templates.

Cutting

All fabrics are strip cut across the width of the fabric from fold to selvage unless otherwise specified, or unless you are using a directional print (cut off all selvages first). Cut the largest pieces first.

FROM QUILTER'S MUSLIN OR CALICO, CUT:

- Seven strips, 22 inches wide. Cross cut into 14 squares. Cross cut each of these squares diagonally and then again to produce 56 quarter-square triangles (48 for the Star blocks and eight for the Half-star blocks).
- Three strips, 10⅞ inches wide. Cross cut into eight squares. Cross cut these on the diagonal to produce 16 half-square triangles for the Half-star blocks.

FROM THE SOLID STAR FABRICS, CUT:

- 10 strips, 11 inches wide.

If you are using the triangle ruler and a rotary cutter: refer to the Cutting Diagram below, and cross cut 12 sets of four matching Template A shapes (48 in all), for the complete Star blocks. Then cut another eight Template A shapes and eight matching mirror-pairs of Template B/BR for the Half-star blocks. Cut also two Template C triangles for every Template A shape (112) and two for each B/BR pair (16), to be used for the points (128 C triangles in all).

If you are not using the ruler: use Templates A, B/BR (flip Template B to obtain the mirror-image BR), and C to cut the shapes, as above.

Cutting Diagram

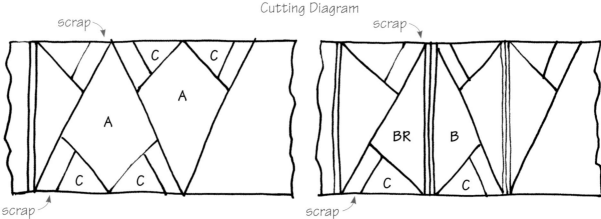

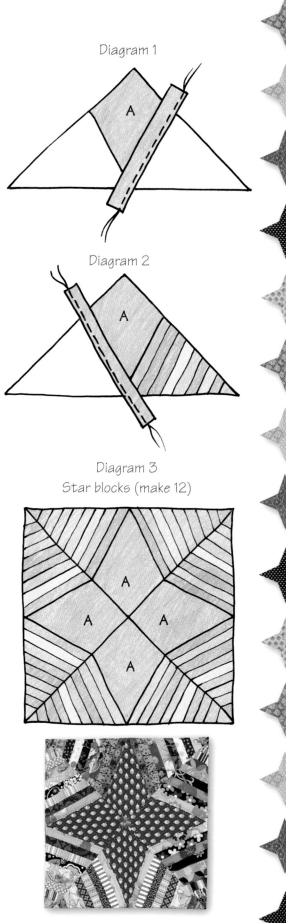

Diagram 1

Diagram 2

Diagram 3
Star blocks (make 12)

SCRAP STRIPS

To select the fabrics for the strips, use your main fabric(s) for the star centers and go through your stash to select colors that relate.

- Cut scraps into 1½-inch strips and separate them into piles of warm and cool strips. Hang them on a hanger or keep them in boxes. As you prepare each block, you may want to trim the strips to the lengths required. The first strip is 10½ inches long and the length decreases by 1 inch per strip for eight strips on each side of the template.

FROM BINDING FABRIC, CUT:

- Eight strips, 2½ inches wide. Join the strips, end to end, using 45-degree seams, and press seams to one side.

Constructing the quilt top

STAR BLOCKS (MAKE 12)

1   Match a Template A shape to a muslin quarter-square triangle. Pin in place, right side up. Start with a contrasting strip and match raw edges with right sides together. Sew a ¼-inch seam through all three layers (Diagram 1). Fold the strip open and press flat without stretching.

2   Continue adding strips in this manner until you have added eight strips, then finish the point with a Template C triangle. Carefully trim any extending edges even with the edge of the foundation triangle. Repeat this process on the opposite side of Template A (Diagram 2). It is a good idea to chain stitch these blocks in sets of four so that you can keep matching star sets together.

DESIGN TIP: *You can randomly sew the strips, or you can also repeat the same pattern for all four triangles. Use a design wall to try out a few strip combinations. After a few squares it will become obvious what you like.*

3   Make a set of four quarter-square triangles for each of the 12 full Star blocks (48 quarter-square triangles in all).

4   When all the quarter-square triangles are complete, sew them together in sets of four to make 12 complete Star blocks (Diagram 3).

HALF-STAR BLOCKS (MAKE 8)

The border is composed of eight Half-star blocks—four on each side. Each Half-star block is composed of a quarter-square triangle flanked by two mirror-image half-square triangles.

5   For each Half-star block, construct a quarter-square triangle, as for Steps 1 and 2 of the Star block, above (eight quarter-square triangles in all).

Diagram 4
Half-star blocks (make 8)

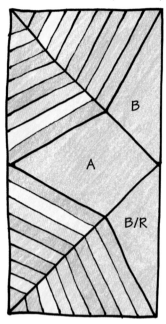

6   Using the 16 half-square muslin triangles as foundation blocks, repeat the process using the B and BR shapes, to give two mirror-image half-square triangles for each of the eight quarter-square triangles (16 half-square triangles in all).

7   Sew a half-square triangle to either side of a quarter-square triangle to make eight Half-star blocks (Diagram 4).

ASSEMBLING THE QUILT TOP

8   Following the Quilt Assembly Diagram and the photographed quilt, lay out the blocks in four rows of three full Star blocks, with a Half-star block on each end. Lay them out on the floor or, preferably, on a design wall for color balancing.

9   Number each row from top to bottom and sew the first block to the second block for all rows, matching all seams. Leave all connecting threads uncut until you have finished with all the rows. Then sew block two to block three for all rows. Join the blocks in this manner until the quilt rows are assembled.

10 Now sew the first row to the second, the second to the third, and so on until finished. Your quilt top is complete!

Quilt Assembly Diagram

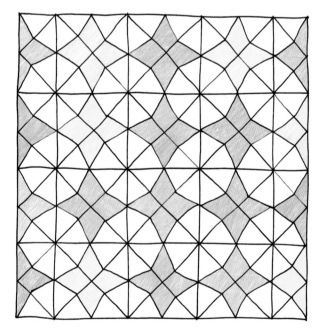

Row 1

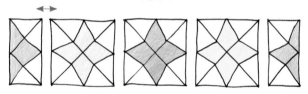

Backing, quilting, and binding

Cut the backing fabric crosswise in half, giving two 90-inch pieces. Remove the selvages and stitch the pieces together up the middle seam. Press the seam open and press the backing piece carefully.

Refer to pages 204–211 for instructions on finishing.

Pop Stars is hand-quilted with perle cotton no. 8 in a variety of colors. The lines work through the strip piecing, each spider web in a different color. The star points are quilted ¼ inch outside the seam lines. When quilting a mad quilt, it is not always necessary to do it by hand, but I love the hyperactivity of this quilt, so I slowed down and, using a number of colors, wove the stitches through the strips of the spider webs, which creates a secondary web design. I followed that theme at the centers of the webs and did a series of large stitches moving out from the center … just for fun.

Maple Leaf Rag

 Sarah Fielke

THE IDEA

This quilt continues to fascinate me because there are so many different ways to make it. There is a bit of everything in this quilt: reproduction, 1930s, spots, stripes, Kaffe Fassett, brights, darks, soft tonal fabrics, scraps from my own quilts, and scraps of quilts made for and by my friends.

Listening to music is something that seems to have woven itself into quite a few quilts in this book. Scott Joplin's piano rag goes around in circles and sounds just how this quilt would sound if it got up and started to play! I can look at the circles and hear the piano dancing in my head, look at the fabrics and see the quilts of my friends and the colors of their laughter. I think it is my favorite quilt ever.

Finished quilt size

Throw, 74 inches square
Block size: 9¾ inches square, including seam allowance

Materials and tools

4⅝ yards quilter's muslin for foundation piecing
Large amount of scraps of fabric of any size, in many different colors and patterns (see Design Tip, below)
Large selection of strips of fabric, at least 3 inches wide
⅝ yard black-and-white-spotted fabric for binding
4½ yards backing fabric
81-inch-square cotton batting (see Design Tip, below)
Template plastic
2B pencil
Rotary cutter, quilter's ruler, and cutting mat
Neutral-colored cotton thread for piecing

DESIGN TIP: *It is impossible to estimate exactly how much fabric is needed. But you will need a lot of scraps to make the crazy pieces in this quilt—it eats fabric! The same goes for the stripped webs. Each web has seven rows of fabric, which comes to more than 350 fabrics. I used a different fabric for every single strip—you need a huge range to make a quilt as scrappy as mine. However, you don't need to make every single web different; feel free to repeat fabrics. But the longer I went on, the more I enjoyed the challenge to find more fabrics! Each of the outer three rows needs two 1½-inch strips to make a full circle. Don't be afraid to use large prints, stripes, checks, and anything else you might usually shy away from. This quilt needs variety to make it interesting. If you run out of fabric options, ask your quilting friends for help. Most will be happy to contribute—all my quilting friends were! If you run out of a fabric halfway around a web, or just before the end, simply add another similar fabric in—I did. It all contributes to the controlled mad jazz that is Maple Leaf Rag.*

I would not normally advise you to buy your batting before you make the quilt. However, if you do not already have a design wall in use for sewing, you will need one for this quilt. Buy your batting first and use it to lay out your blocks as you piece. If you can put the batting up on the wall, that is ideal, but if you can't, laying it out on a bed is fine too. Pin the blocks to the batting background and carefully roll it up when you have to put it away, which will save you having to reorganize every web each time you get the quilt out.

NOTE: *It is recommended that all fabrics be 100 percent cotton, and be ironed. Requirements are based on fabric 44 inches wide. Unless otherwise stated, all seam allowances are ¼ inch throughout. Color test any dark fabrics that you are using (see page 189), and wash them before cutting if they run.*
    Please read all instructions before starting.

Templates

Trace the pattern for Template A (on pattern sheet) onto template plastic using a 2B pencil and cut out using sharp scissors—not fabric scissors!

Cutting

All fabrics are strip cut across the width of the fabric from fold to selvage unless otherwise specified, or unless you are using a directional print (cut off all selvages first). Cut the largest pieces first.

FROM QUILTER'S MUSLIN, CUT:

• 16 strips, 10¼ inches wide. Cross cut into 64 squares, each 10¼ inches. Cut each square in half on the diagonal, giving 128 half-square triangles, for the strip-pieced units.

FROM THE STRIPS OF FABRIC, CUT:

• A variety of strips, 1½ inches wide. You will need two full strips for each of the outer three fabrics in each full web, and one strip each from the other four. For the half-webs, you will need one strip of each fabric.

FROM BLACK-AND-WHITE-SPOTTED FABRIC, CUT:

• Eight strips, 2½ inches wide, for the binding. Join the strips, end to end, using 45-degree seams, and press seams to one side.

Constructing the quilt top

CRAZY-PIECED UNITS

1 Following Diagram 1, place two scraps together at an angle, right sides together, and sew. Trim any excess away to a neat ¼-inch seam

allowance. Flip the pieces open and finger-press the seam. Arrange another scrap in the same manner in a different direction (Diagram 2). Continue like this until you have made a large piece of crazy-pieced fabric. You can also make several small pieces of different patterns or strips and sew them all together.

2   When the piece is large enough, press it thoroughly, and ensure that all the seams are flat. Place Template A on top of the piece and trace around the shape as many times as you can fit with a sharp 2B pencil (Diagram 3). Cut the units out using scissors or a rotary cutter.

3   Continue in this manner until you have made 128 crazy-pieced Template A shapes. You can add any scraps left over from cutting the first pieces onto the next crazy fabric you make. Take care to store the pieces somewhere flat, where they cannot be stretched out of shape and require lots of ironing before being sewn into the quilt.

TIP: *"Pressing" means placing the iron on top of the block and pressing down—not sliding the iron back and forth. There are so many seams in this quilt that ironing rather than pressing will result in stretching, making the quilt difficult to put together.*

STRIP-PIECED UNITS

Now things get a little tricky! Try to be very organized as you complete each section so that you form webs and grow the quilt in different directions. I pick out all seven fabrics for the web I am building at once and arrange them into a color grade I'm happy with. I ensure there are enough strips cut from each fabric to get around the web, then hang them from a coat hanger close to my sewing machine. When I get to a place where I have several webs all half-pieced at once, I have all the fabrics for each web organized on a hanger, within reach, ready for the next block.

4   Take a muslin half-square triangle. Place a Template A crazy-pieced unit onto the muslin, right side up. The square corner of the unit matches the square corner of the triangle (Diagram 4).

5   Place the first strip of your web on top of the Template A piece with the raw edges aligned, right sides together, and sew through all three layers. Flip the strip open to cover part of the muslin and finger-press the seam flat. Lay the next strip on top of the first strip, right sides together and raw edges aligned, and sew. Flip this strip open and finger-press. Take care as you progress that the edges of the strips are covering the muslin template. Continue in this manner until you have sewn seven strips onto the muslin (Diagram 5, page 128).

6   Press the triangle carefully and trim the strips back to be the same size as the muslin template. Put these trimmed strips aside for the next part of the block and take up a different set.

Diagram 1

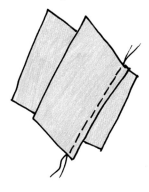

Diagram 2

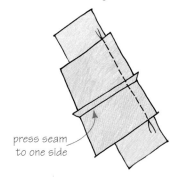

press seam
to one side

Diagram 3

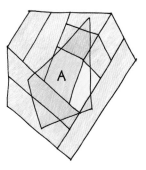

Diagram 4

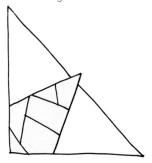

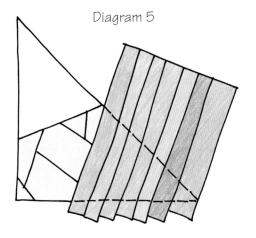

Diagram 5

7 Repeat the process to cover the other side of the half-square triangle with the different set of strips. Press and trim (Diagram 6).

8 Place the resulting completed triangle onto your design wall, positioned at the top left-hand corner of the quilt. You will now need to make the other triangle to complete the other half of the square in the block. It will be a mirror-image of the triangle you have just pieced. Join the two triangles up the center to form a square block (Diagram 7).

9 Continue piecing until you have made 64 blocks, eight squares across and eight down. Refer to Diagram 8 as you piece, noting which web you are piecing and where in the pattern you are up to, although if you lay the quilt out as you go, you'll soon see if you make a mistake!

ASSEMBLING THE QUILT TOP

10 Sew the blocks into eight rows of eight across the quilt. Make sure you keep them in order as you go—don't ruin all that hard organizing work! The best thing to do is to lay out the entire quilt on the floor or on the design wall and pick the blocks up in rows to sew; that way, you can't go wrong. (There are a lot of lumpy points to go together in the center of these webs; take care to press your seams in opposite directions on each row to reduce the bulk.) Your quilt top is complete!

Backing, quilting, and binding

Cut the backing fabric crosswise in half into two 81-inch pieces. Remove the selvages and stitch the pieces together up the middle seam. Press the seam allowance open and press the backing piece carefully.

Refer to pages 204–211 for instructions on finishing.

Maple Leaf Rag is machine-quilted with a neutral cream thread in a pattern that echoes the swirls and circles in the quilt so that it does not compete with the piecing.

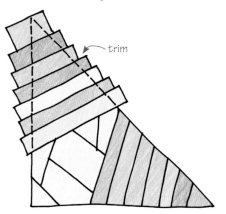

Diagram 6

trim

Diagram 7

Diagram 8

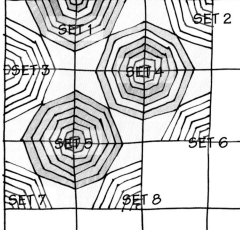

SET 1 SET 2
SET 3 SET 4
SET 5 SET 6
SET 7 SET 8

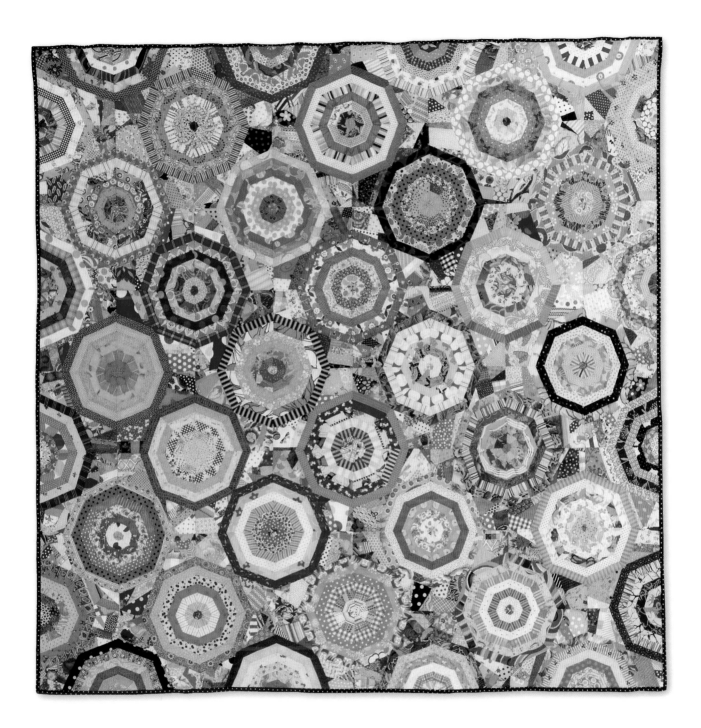

Shared Inspiration

Mixed technique quilts are a fun challenge. They may seem tricky but in actual fact are not as hard as they look. The stripped units are foundation-pieced (similar to a Wedding Ring or Pickle Dish block) and then appliquéd onto a background square. Foundation-piecing allows for smaller piecing, interesting angles, and bias control, and it is a great way to make a tricky quilt come together more easily and with greater accuracy.

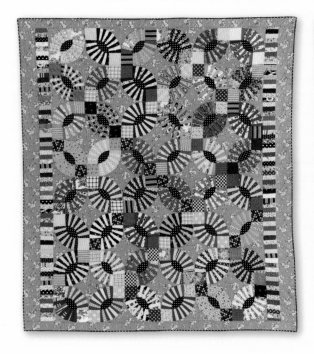

Fruit Tingles

Gypsy Kisses

Gypsy Kisses

 Kathy Doughty

THE IDEA

Okay, it was my dream: rainy afternoon over coffee, leafing through quilt books with Kaffe Fassett! It was in a real moment, doing just that, when he pointed to a photo of this pattern in black and white. I was immediately captivated by the graphic impact of the quilt. Foundation-piecing was new to me, but I drafted the block and then carefully took out my most beloved fabric (a fabric I loved so much I bought the bolt!) to make this quilt. It is my all-time favorite quilt, as much for the finished product as for how it began.

Foundation-piecing is a handy trick to learn. The lined paper allows you to control bias and to be accurate when using smaller pieces or odd-shaped scraps. Give it a try and you may end up hooked like me!

Finished quilt size

King, 93 x 102½ inches
Block size: 24½ inches, including seam allowance

Materials and tools

5⅝ yards background fabric

4 yards light scrap strips at least 5½ inches wide, for foundation strips

4 yards dark scrap strips at least 5½ inches wide, for foundation strips

1⅝ yards black-and-white-spotted fabric for "eye" centers and binding

¾ yard in total of a variety of medium-value light scraps, at least 4½ inches wide, for squares

¾ yard in total of a variety of medium-value dark scraps, at least 4½ inches wide, for squares

100 x 110 inches cotton batting

9 yards backing fabric

Template plastic, 2B pencil, and silver gel pen

96 sheets foundation paper (see Foundation-piecing on page 196)

Rotary cutter, quilter's ruler, and cutting mat

Appliqué needles

Black sewing thread for appliqué

Masking tape

Spray starch

Neutral-colored cotton thread for piecing

Sulky 12 cotton thread for quilting

DESIGN TIP: *For the background, select a fabric that has a retro feel to it with medium-sized, all-over graphics. It should set the tone for the quilt and allow you to use a variety of colors, including black. For the blades of the crescent, select fabrics that are varied in value, from very strong to medium. Include blacks! This is a great scrap quilt, so don't be afraid to make substitutions*

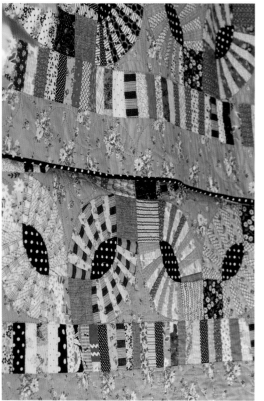

along the way. For the "eye" centers, select a strong dark color that will make these pieces hold the "eye" together. The joining squares are more neutral and should not compete with the crescent shapes.

NOTE: *It is recommended that all fabrics be 100 percent cotton, and be ironed. Requirements are based on fabric 44 inches wide. Unless otherwise stated, all seam allowances are ¼ inch throughout. Color test any dark fabrics that you are using (see page 189), and wash them before cutting if they run.*
    Please read all instructions before starting.

Templates

Trace the pattern for Template A (on the pattern sheet) onto template plastic using a 2B pencil, and cut out using sharp scissors—not fabric scissors! Photocopy or trace the Foundation Template (on the pattern sheet) 96 times onto foundation paper. Trim paper to edge of lines. The template will be the exact size needed for the finished shape, so be sure to leave seam allowance beyond all sides of the paper when sewing the fabric.

Cutting

All fabrics are strip cut across the width of the fabric from fold to selvage unless otherwise specified, or unless you are using a directional print (cut off all selvages first). Cut the largest pieces first. Save all scraps for the pieced border.

FROM BACKGROUND FABRIC, CUT:
- One piece, approximately 100 inches long, along the length, and set aside for Side Edges and Outer Borders, which will be cut to size when the foundation-piecing is completed.
- Six strips (across width of remaining fabric), each 13½ inches wide. Cross cut these strips into 18 squares, each 13½ inches.
- One square, 16¼ inches. Cross cut on the diagonal twice to make four quarter-square triangles for the top and bottom edges.

FROM DARK AND LIGHT FOUNDATION STRIP FABRICS, CUT:
- A series of strips, 2½ x 5½ inches. Each double crescent consists of 12 dark strips and 10 light strips (22 strips in all). Cut enough for 48 sets of double crescents. Feel free to make substitutions of equal value along the way for a more antique look.

FROM LIGHT AND DARK MEDIUM-VALUE SCRAPS, CUT:

- A series of strips, 4½ inches wide. Cross cut into two squares of each fabric, until you have 48 pairs of matching squares (96 squares in all). These squares should be of medium value so as not to compete with the crescent shapes.

FROM BLACK-AND-WHITE-SPOTTED FABRIC, CUT:

- Five strips, 4½ inches wide. Using a sharp 2B pencil or a gel pen, trace 48 Template A "eye" shapes onto the right side of the fabric, and cut out, adding a scant ¼-inch seam allowance all around.
- 10 strips, 2½ inches wide, for binding. Join the strips, end to end, using 45-degree seams, and press seams to one side.

FROM LEFTOVER SCRAPS OF FABRICS, CUT:

- A series of strips, 2 x 5 inches (you will need about 130 strips). Join together along the 5-inch edges to make two borders, approximately 96½ inches long.

Constructing the quilt top

The quilt is constructed of 12 blocks. Each block consists of eight crescent shapes (four double crescents), four center "eyes," eight 4½-inch squares, and one 13½-inch background square.

FOUNDATION-PIECING FOR CRESCENTS

1 Refer to Foundation-piecing on page 196. Match the cut foundation strips in sets of 22, each with 10 light and 12 dark strips.

2 Align a light and a dark strip, right sides together, and position them on the back of a foundation paper crescent with the dark color closest to the paper and the sewing lines on the paper facing up. By holding the paper up to the light, you can see the stitching line and can therefore position the fabric so that it extends ¼ inch over the first sewing line.

3 Sew in place through all layers, using a small (1.5) stitch length (Diagram 1). Use an old sewing machine needle, as the paper dulls the needle. The fabric strips will be larger than the template. This is your seam allowance; do not trim yet.

4 Finger-press (or iron) the contrast (light) fabric open. To establish the next seam, fold the foundation paper along the next sewing line and trim the extending strip ¼ inch beyond the seam. Flatten out the paper again and, on the wrong side as before, position the next strip of fabric, alternating dark and light, to match the cut line, right sides together.

5 Continue piecing along each of the lines, alternating light and dark strips (Diagram 2), until the paper is covered. Trim both curved edges and the first and last straight edges to a neat ¼-inch seam allowance.

Diagram 1

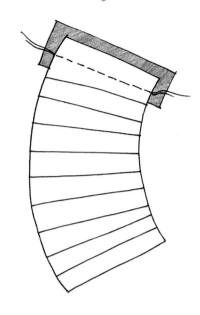

Diagram 2

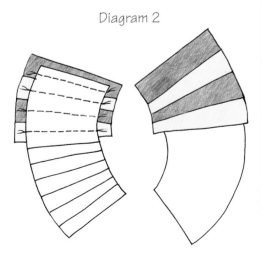

Diagram 3

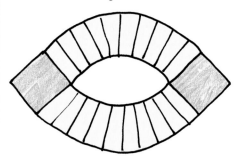

Diagram 4

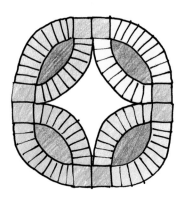

Diagram 5

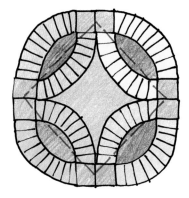

Repeat this process with a second foundation paper and the remaining 11 strips, for the matching side.

6 Repeat the process until you have made 48 double sets in this manner.

TIP: *When foundation-piecing, it is handy to have an ironing board set up next to the sewing machine so that pressing is conveniently nearby.*

JOINING THE CRESCENTS

7 Match two matching squares to each set of crescents. The square should line up with the raw trimmed straight edge of the crescent. Sew a square to each end of one crescent section, sewing along the edge of the paper, then sew the remaining crescent in the set to the other side of the squares, thus joining the two halves to complete the double crescent shape with an "eye" hole in the middle (Diagram 3).

"EYE" CENTER APPLIQUÉ

8 Appliqué the "eye" centers in place on the double crescents, using your preferred method of appliqué (see page 198).

ASSEMBLING THE BLOCKS

9 Lay out the double crescents in sets of four. Match the squares together, pin, and sew in place. Repeat to form a unit of four double crescents in a "donut" shape (Diagram 4). Repeat to make 12 donuts.

10 Fold a background square in half on the diagonal, and then in half again, and press the folds. Open out and use masking tape to secure it to a tabletop or the back of a cutting mat, setting it on point.

11 Press the seam allowance to the back of the donut unit on the edge that will be appliquéd. To do this, fold the fabric over to the wrong side using the foundation paper as a guide, spray starch, and then press.

12 Carefully tear away the foundation paper from the back of this side only. Pinch the unit in your hands and gently tear or use a seam ripper. It helps to fold back the paper a few times. Match the pieced unit to the background square so that the fold creases coincide with the points formed where the squares meet (Diagram 5). Be sure that there is enough background material at the points to safely appliqué the unit onto the background. Baste the units in place onto the background squares, and then appliqué in place (see page 198). Repeat this process for all 12 donuts.

13 Now lay your donuts out in four horizontal rows of three. With right sides together, sew Donut 1 to Donut 2 across the adjacent squares, then join Donut 3 to Donut 2 in the same way. Repeat for each of the four rows.

14 Now join the rows together in the same way, by stitching adjacent squares together, as before (Diagram 6).

15 You now need to apply the remaining six background squares (numbered 1 to 6 on Diagram 7) to the "holes" created in the center of the quilt top by the joining of the rows. This stage is a bit awkward. It helps to lay out the quilt on a large, flat surface and slide the background squares (attached to a movable hard surface) in place to baste and then appliqué, in the same manner as before.

16 Measure the quilt top through the center in both directions. It should measure 72½ x 96½ inches. If your measurements differ, adjust your Side Edges accordingly.

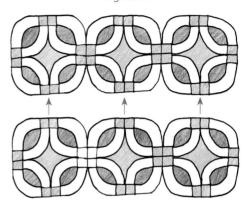

Diagram 6

ADDING SIDE EDGE STRIPS AND TRIANGLES

17 Take the reserved length of background fabric and cut two strips, along the length, each 8¼ x 96½ inches, for the Side Edges. (Set remaining fabric aside.)

18 To fill the triangular gaps at the sides of the quilt top, pin or baste the Side Edge strips underneath the side edges of the quilt top (Diagram 7) and then appliqué. (A single long strip rather than individual triangles helps to prevent bias stretch on quilt edges.)

19 Finally, baste the four quarter-square background triangles in position underneath the top and bottom edges of the quilt top (see Diagram 7) and appliqué in place.

20 Once all the appliqué is complete, you can cut away the excess background fabric from behind the quilt top, to reduce bulk and make quilting easier. Measure your quilt top through the center in both directions. It should measure 72½ x 96½ inches. If your measurements differ, adjust your border measurements.

Diagram 7

PIECED BORDERS

21 Trim the pieced border strips to match the sides of your quilt. Find the middle of the border strip and the middle of the side of the quilt top and pin in place. Match the ends, pin, and then carefully pin the length of the strip to the quilt top. Sew in place and repeat for opposite side. Measure your quilt top through the center in both directions. It should measure 81½ x 96½ inches.

OUTER BORDERS

22 Take the remaining length of reserved fabric and, cutting along the length, cut two strips, each 6¼ x 96½ inches, for side borders, and two strips, each 3½ x 93 inches, for top and bottom borders.

23 Find the middle of one side border strip and the middle of the side of the quilt top and pin in place. Match the ends, and then carefully pin

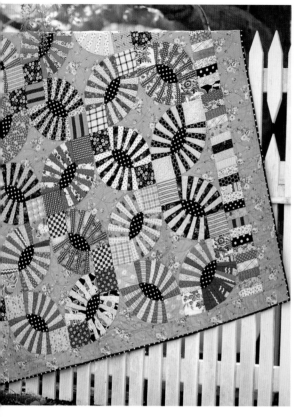

the length of the strip to the quilt top. Sew in place and repeat for the opposite side.

24 Pin and sew the top and bottom borders in the same way. Your quilt top is complete!

Backing, quilting, and binding

Cut the backing fabric crosswise into three 108-inch pieces. Remove the selvages and stitch the pieces together. Press the seam allowances open and press the backing piece carefully.

Refer to pages 204–211 for instructions on finishing.

The quilting for a traditional quilt like Gypsy Kisses required a bit of thought. I reduced the size of my usual perle cotton no. 8 to Sulky machine-embroidery cotton, even though I was hand-quilting, as I wanted slightly smaller stitches for authenticity. I chose this to maintain an old-fashioned look to the quilt. The quilting lines are on the down side of the foundation-pieced strips, with the quilting lines going through the blades on the side without seam allowance, around the "eyes," and echoing the seams in the squares. I then used the template from the "eyes" and chalk-marked it in a four-petal flower shape onto the center background squares with the points of the template meeting at the middle. I then repeated the template shape in each of the four-patch squares and around the borders.

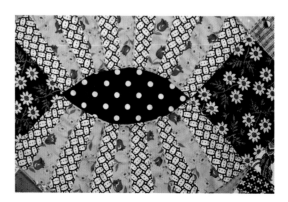

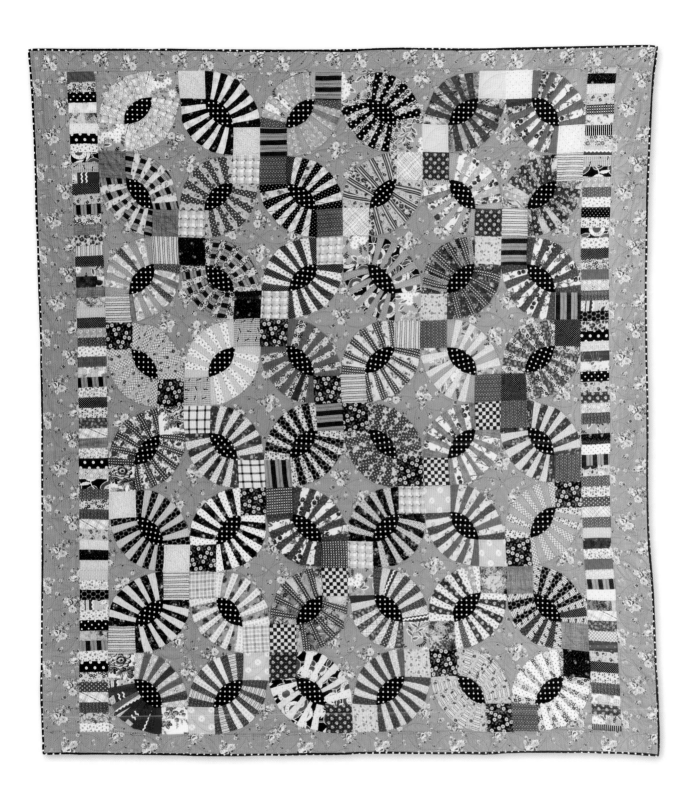

Fruit Tingles

 Sarah Fielke

THE IDEA

When I was a kid, Fruit Tingles was the name of my favorite candy—pretty, colored candies that fizzed on the end of your tongue. Similarly, the jagged ellipses used in this quilt seem to fizz their colors around the central floral and create a great energy.

This quilt is an exercise in color grading. It's important to choose your shades carefully and use them wisely, to create the slightly throbbing effect of the points around the circles. Don't be afraid to use lots of different-size prints in the piecing of the ellipses; you will have much more interesting results if you use both large- and small-scale fabrics, creating more movement in the colors.

Finished quilt size

Double, 84½ inches square

Materials and tools

¼ yard each of 9 different light red and 9 different dark red fabrics

¼ yard each of 9 different light blue and 9 different dark blue fabrics

¼ yard each of 9 different light green and 9 different dark green fabrics

¼ yard each of 9 different light orange and 9 different dark orange fabrics

⅞ yard black-and-white-spotted fabric

6⅝ yards large floral-print fabric for background and border

Foundation paper or photocopier paper (see Foundation-piecing on page 196)

7⅞ yards backing fabric

90-inch-square cotton batting

Silver gel pen

Appliqué glue (optional)

Black cotton thread and appliqué needles

Rotary cutter, quilter's ruler, and cutting mat

Masking tape (optional)

Neutral-colored cotton thread for piecing

NOTE: *It is recommended that all fabrics be 100 percent cotton, and be ironed. Requirements are based on fabric 44 inches wide. Unless otherwise stated, all seam allowances are ¼ inch throughout. Color test any dark fabrics that you are using (see page 189), and wash them before cutting if they run.*

Please read all instructions before starting.

Templates

The circle template (A) and foundation shapes are on the pattern sheet. Trace Template A onto template plastic using a sharp 2B pencil and cut out using sharp scissors—not fabric scissors! Photocopy or trace the foundation shapes onto foundation paper or photocopier paper. You will need 36 copies of Foundation Shape 1 (Ellipsis) and four copies of Foundation Shape 2 (Corner Fan), each with all the markings. Trim the paper on both shapes to approximately ¼ inch outside the lines.

Cutting

All fabrics are strip cut across the width of the fabric from fold to selvage unless otherwise specified, or unless you are using a directional print (cut off all selvages first). Cut the largest pieces first. Although we specify border measurements in the Cutting directions, it is advisable not to cut your border strips accurately until you have constructed the quilt top.

FROM EACH OF THE 72 LIGHT AND DARK FABRICS, CUT:

- One strip, 3½ inches wide. Cross cut into six pieces, each 6½ inches long, for the Foundation Shape 1 piecing. (Note that this will give you some pieces that are too big for some of the spaces, but it does give you freedom to place the colors wherever you please as you piece.)

FROM REMAINING LIGHT AND DARK FABRIC, CUT:

- 32 rectangles, 3½ x 14½ inches, for the Corner Fan squares.
- 124 squares, each 2½ inches, for Border 2.

FROM FLORAL BACKGROUND FABRIC, CUT:

- Seven strips, 14½ inches wide, for the blocks. Cross cut into 13 squares, each 14½ inches.
- Six strips, 1½ inches wide, for Border 1.
- A piece of fabric, 60 inches along the length. From this length, you will need four strips, approximately 58½ x 10½ inches, for the edges of the quilt center. But do not cut these strips accurately until you have pieced the rest of the quilt center, as your measurements may differ.
- A piece of fabric, approximately 64½ inches along the length, for Border 3. Do not cut this length until you have pieced the rest of the quilt center, as your measurements may come out slightly differently.

FROM THE BLACK-AND-WHITE-SPOTTED FABRIC, CUT:

- 10 strips, 2½ inches wide, for binding. Join the strips, end to end, using 45-degree seams, and press seams to one side.
- 24 circles, using Template A and a silver gel pen. Cut out the circles, ¼ inch outside the silver line, and set aside for appliqué.

Constructing the quilt top

FOUNDATION-PIECING

Make all the foundations for each color at the same time.

1   Take the strips you cut for each color and lay them near your sewing machine in piles of light and dark. Your Foundation Shape 1 papers have numbered markings on them, which refer to the order of piecing. They also refer to the light/dark placement, that is, on each piece 1 is dark, 2 is light, and so on.

2   Begin by laying a dark and light piece, right sides together and with raw edges matching, at the back of the foundation paper. You can hold it up to the light to make sure that the fabric is in the right position. It should be lying with the dark side to the paper, and the raw edges along the dotted edge line for piece 1.

3   Pin, if desired. I don't pin when foundation-piecing, as I find that the paper is distorted, but if you feel more comfortable pinning, then do.

4   Sew along the unbroken line through all three layers. Turn the paper over and flip the fabrics open. Make sure that you have covered the whole of the shape before attaching the next one. To check that this is happening, it is useful to fold the fabrics open a bit before you sew to check where they will fall. Press.

5   Lay the next piece of fabric on top of the last fabric and check the placement as before. Sew. If there is any excess fabric past the seam after sewing that is more than ¼ inch, fold the paper back and trim the seam to ¼ inch, otherwise your quilt will become very bulky.

6   Continue until you have covered the whole shape, alternating light and dark fabrics as you go. Press, and then trim the fabric and the paper shape to match the outer line of the shape. Put aside.

7   Make nine ellipses of each color in the same way, giving a total of 36 ellipses.

8   When you have finished all the ellipse shapes, repeat this process using the Corner Fan Foundation Shapes and make four Corner Fan units. Alternate the fabrics randomly; they do not have to be light/dark. Press and set aside.

ASSEMBLING THE QUILT TOP

9   Fold a 14¼-inch square into quarters on the diagonal and finger-press the creases in. Following the photograph of the quilt, arrange the ellipses by color. Take the four ellipses for the first circle (which should be blue, red, green, orange, starting at the top left-hand ellipse and working clockwise) and remove the foundation paper. Turn the square on point and place the ellipses onto the square with the points of the ellipses covering the points of the square. Make sure that the ellipses are arranged evenly, using the diagonal creases as a guide.

Diagram 1

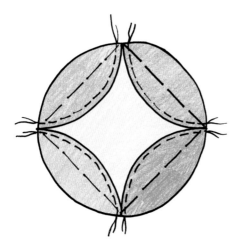

Diagram 2

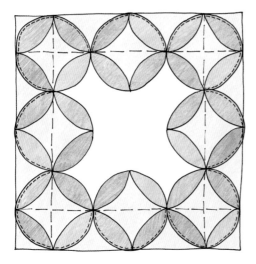

Hand-baste each ellipse to the background square using small basting stitches, just over ¼ inch inside the silver gel pen line (Diagram 1).

10 Using a neutral thread, turn the edge of the ellipses under along the silver gel pen line and hand-appliqué in place (see page 198). When you have appliquéd all four ellipses, remove the basting stitches. Turn the piece over and carefully cut away the excess background fabric, approximately ½ inch from the seam line. Press gently and set aside somewhere flat.

11 Repeat with the next circle until you have appliquéd nine circles, three across the quilt and three down.

12 Arrange the circles on the floor in order and measure through the center in both directions. It should measure 58½ inches square including seam allowance, but if your measurements differ, remember to adjust your edge strips accordingly.

13 Cut four edge strips, 58½ x 10 inches (or your desired measurement). Lift the edges of the outer circles and slip a 58½ x 10½-inch strip underneath the edges, overlapping the ends to form a square "frame." Use masking tape to secure these strips in place in a perfect square.

14 Replace the circles over the top of the border strips and arrange them so that they are just over ¼ inch in from the edge of the strip. Baste the edges of the outer circles down carefully (Diagram 2).

15 Remove the center circle and place the four remaining background squares on point in the middle of the quilt. Position the squares using the diagonal creases as a guide, as before. Replace the last circle, position carefully, and baste all the edges down firmly (Diagram 3). Remove masking tape.

16 Needle-turn appliqué all the remaining edges of the ellipses in place. Don't worry about what happens when the points of the ellipses come together, as they will be covered by the black-and-white circles.

17 Cut away the excess background fabric, as before, approximately ½ inch from the seam line. Trim the borders to be ¼ inch from the edge of the ellipses and ensure the quilt top is square. Measure the top through the center in both directions. It should measure 58½ inches square.

BORDER 1 (FLORAL)

18 Take the 1½-inch strips of floral fabric, remove the selvages, and sew the strips together, end to end, into one long strip.

19 If, like mine, your top doesn't measure exactly 58½ inches square (nobody's perfect!), cut two pieces for the top and bottom borders of the quilt to the actual measurement. Pin the center of the strip and the center of the quilt top together, pin the ends, and then pin in between. Sew and repeat with the opposite end.

Diagram 3

20 Measure the quilt through the center in the other direction and cut the remaining border pieces to that measurement. Repeat Step 19 to attach the remaining borders. The quilt top should now measure 60½ inches square (if your original measurement was 58½ inches).

21 Now that Border 1 is attached, you can appliqué the black-and-white circles in place, as some of them extend onto the border.

APPLIQUÉ

22 Finger-press on the gel line around each black-and-white circle. Place a circle over the join of each of the ellipses and attach with a dab of appliqué glue. Wait for the glue to dry, and then needle-turn appliqué the circles in place using black cotton.

BORDER 2 (PIECED)

23 Sew together four strips of 2½-inch squares in random color arrangements. Two strips should be 30 squares long and two should be 32 squares long. If your quilt center was not 58½ inches finished, you may have to play with this measurement to make your squares fit. (Slightly adjust the measurement of squares within the rows if you need to, but keep the corners correct.)

24 Pin the center of one of the shorter strips to the top of the quilt, pin the ends, and then pin in between and sew. Repeat with the bottom border. Repeat with the two longer side borders, matching the points of the squares at the corners. The quilt top should now measure 64½ inches square through the center. If your measurements differ, remember to adjust your borders accordingly.

BORDER 3 (FLORAL)

25 Cut the remaining floral background fabric to 64½ inches long. From this length of fabric, cut four strips, 10½ x 64½ inches, for Border 3.

26 Sew a foundation-pieced Corner Fan square to either end of two of the strips, with the sharp points of the fan pointing in toward quilt.

27 Find the center of one of the shorter strips and the center of the top of the quilt, pin the centers and then the ends, and then in between, and sew. Repeat with the bottom border, and then repeat to attach both the side borders with the Corner Fan squares attached. Your quilt top is complete!

Backing, quilting, and binding

Cut the backing fabric crosswise into three pieces, each 94 inches. Remove the selvages and stitch the pieces together up the lengthwise seams. Press the seam allowances open and press the backing piece carefully.

Refer to pages 204–211 for instructions on finishing.

Fruit Tingles was machine-quilted in a large, swirling pattern using cream-colored thread.

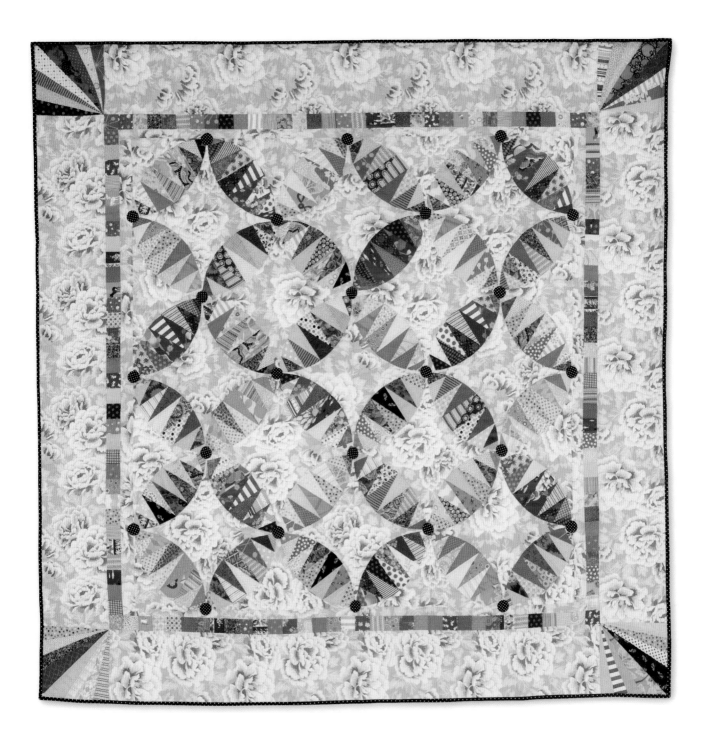

Shared Inspiration

Birds are often seen in quilts, as our quilting sisters before us used images seen from their window as inspiration. There are elaborate birds and simple birds, but they often make a quilt sing. We chose to do one quilt each, with a medallion of birds and mixed, pieced, and fabric borders. Looking Back is traditionally inspired and delicate in nature, while Bluebirds & Happiness is a bit more simplistic and contemporary in nature.

Looking Back

Bluebirds & Happiness

Bluebirds & Happiness

 Kathy Doughty

THE IDEA

Is there a happier sound than birds chirping outside the window? Their lightness and clever-colored feathers have made them features in quilts throughout time. I am relatively new to appliqué, so I like my shapes to be simple but effective. Circles, birds, and leaves are easy and fun! Combine that with a few border tricks, and happiness is a quilt with bluebirds! The circles in the borders are loosely fussy-cut to utilize the patterns in the fabric. Circular motifs are not hard to find. You can use a graphic image, as I did, or choose one with pictures of flowers, or even birds. As for the border, again the quilt group gasped, but I like a plaid and this one pulls the colors from the medallion all the way out to the binding.

Finished quilt size
Double, 86½ x 88½ inches

Materials and tools
⅔ yard fabric for Center Medallion
½ yard blue-floral fabric for Border 1
3⅛ yards light-patterned fabric for Borders 2, 4, and 6
½ yard patterned-striped fabric for Border 3
1 yard narrow-striped fabric for Borders 2, 4, and 6
1⅛ yards dark plum fabric for Borders 4 and 5
2¼ yards different fabrics (in total) with circular or floral motifs for the appliqué in the borders
1⅓ yards plaid or checked fabric for Border 7
⅛ yard each of blue, brown, and orange fabric for the Birds, Wings, and Flowers
2 yards brown ¼-inch-wide self-adhesive bias quilting tape
⅔ yard fabric for binding
7⅔ yards backing fabric
98-inch-square batting
Template plastic
Silver gel pen
Appliqué needles
Appliqué glue
Rotary cutter, quilter's ruler, and cutting mat
Neutral-colored cotton thread for piecing
Cotton thread to match appliqué fabrics
2B pencil

NOTE: *It is recommended that all fabrics be 100 percent cotton, and be ironed. Requirements are based on fabric 44 inches wide. Unless otherwise stated, all seam allowances are ¼ inch throughout. Color test any dark fabrics that you are using (see page 189), and wash them before cutting if they run.*
    Please read all instructions before starting.

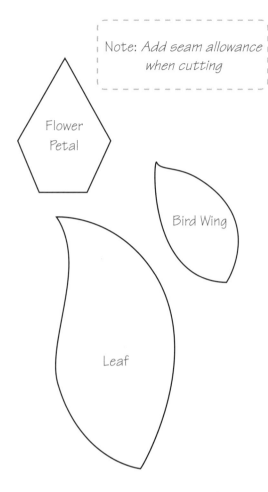

Note: *Add seam allowance when cutting*

Flower Petal

Bird Wing

Leaf

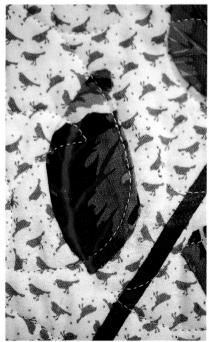

Templates

The smaller templates are on these pages. The seven circular Flower Centers are on the pattern sheet. Trace all the appliqué shapes (Flower Petal, seven Flower Centers, Leaf, Bird, Eye, Wing) onto template plastic using a sharp 2B pencil. Cut out all shapes accurately using sharp scissors—not fabric scissors! Label your templates.

Cutting

All fabrics are strip cut across the width of the fabric from fold to selvage unless otherwise specified, or unless you are using a directional print (cut off all selvages first). Cut the largest pieces first.

FROM BACKGROUND MEDALLION FABRIC, CUT:
- One 21½-inch square.

FROM BLUE-FLORAL FABRIC, CUT:
- One strip, 4¾ inches wide. Cross cut into two strips, each 4¾ x 21½ inches, for top and bottom of Border 1.
- One strip, 3¾ inches wide. Cross cut into two strips, each 3¾ x 30 inches, for sides of Border 1.
- Four squares, each 3¼ inches, for corners of Border 3.
- Four squares, each 2½ inches, for corners of Border 5.

FROM NARROW-STRIPED FABRIC, CUT:
- Four strips, 2 inches wide. Set aside for Border 2.
- Four strips, 2½ inches wide. Cross cut these into 54 squares, each 2½ inches, for pieced Border 4.
- Seven strips, 2 inches wide. Join end to end and set aside for Border 6.

FROM LIGHT-PATTERNED FABRIC, CUT:
- Eight strips, 3 inches wide. Set aside for Border 2.
- Nine strips, 2½ inches wide. Cross cut into 54 squares, each 2½ inches, and 26 rectangles, 2½ x 6½ inches, for pieced Border 4.
- 14 strips, 3½ inches wide. Join end to end and set aside for Border 6.

FROM PATTERNED-STRIPED FABRIC, CUT:
- Four strips, 3¼ inches wide. Set aside for Border 3.

FROM DARK PLUM FABRIC, CUT:
- Nine strips, 2½ inches wide. Cross cut into 54 squares, each 2½ inches, and 26 rectangles, 2½ x 6½ inches, for pieced Border 4.
- Six strips, 2½ inches wide. Join these end to end and set aside for Border 5.

FROM PLAID FABRIC, CUT:

- Eight strips, 5 inches wide. Join these end to end and set aside for Border 7.

FROM BINDING FABRIC, CUT:

- Nine strips, 2½ inches wide. Join the strips, end to end, using 45-degree seams, and press seams to one side.

APPLIQUÉ FABRICS

Use the templates to trace the appliqué shapes onto the front of the fabrics with a silver gel pen. Trace and cut the pieces as follows, cutting a scant ¼ inch outside the traced line:

- Four floral motif 7½-inch Circles
- 16 floral motif 6-inch Circles
- 16 floral motif 4-inch Circles
- Four floral motif 3½-inch Circles
- One orange 6-inch Circle
- Six orange 2½-inch Circles
- Seven blue 1½-inch Circles
- Six brown 1-inch Circles
- Seven brown Flower Petals
- 17 green Leaves
- Six blue Birds
- Six brown Wings
- Six black spots for Eyes

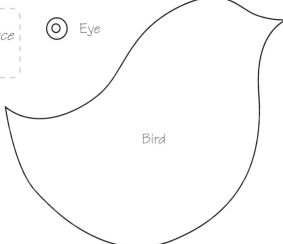

Note: *Add seam allowance when cutting*

 Eye

Bird

Constructing the quilt top

CENTER MEDALLION APPLIQUÉ

Read the instructions for Appliqué on page 198 before proceeding.

1. For the Center Medallion, you will need: one orange 6-inch Circle, seven blue 1½-inch Circles, six orange 2½-inch Circles, six brown 1-inch Circles, seven brown Flower Petals, 17 green Leaves, six blue Birds, six brown Wings, six black spots for Eyes.

2. From the bias quilting tape, cut one 15-inch piece for the main stem, one 11-inch piece for the top stem, one 17-inch piece for the middle stem, and one 22-inch piece for the bottom stem.

3. Finger-press the seam allowance to the wrong side along the gel pen line.

4. Fold the Center Medallion fabric into thirds across the width and the length. Use the folds to help place the cut-out shapes and bias tape in position, following the photograph. Use appliqué glue to hold the appliqué pieces in place, and then appliqué them down, starting with the smaller pieces that sit on top, and working to the bottom layer before attaching the completed pieces to the background square.

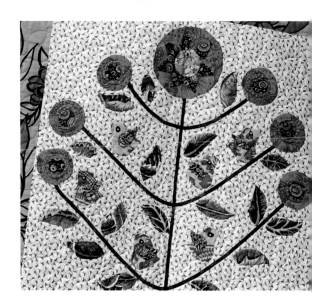

BORDER 1 (BLUE-FLORAL)

5 First sew the top and bottom (shorter) Border 1 strips to the top and bottom of the Center Medallion. Pin the centers and then the ends of the strips and sew them in place.

6 Add the side borders. The top should now measure 28 x 30 inches.

BORDER 2 (APPLIQUÉD CIRCLES)

7 Take the four narrow-striped strips for Border 2 and cross cut to make two strips, each 2 x 28 inches, and two strips, each 2 x 43 inches. Take the eight light-patterned strips for Border 2 and cross cut to make four strips, each 3 x 28 inches, and four strips, each 3 x 43 inches.

8 Sort the Border 2 strips into two matching sets of three strips (light/stripe/light) for each of the two different cut lengths. Sew the strips together along the length, giving four stripped borders. Press the seams to the dark side. The appliqué is best done at this stage, before sewing the borders in place.

9 Fold the joined strips in half crosswise and in half again. Press the folds and use the pressed lines as markers for placing your appliquéd circles, using the photograph as a guide. The shorter (top and bottom) borders each have four evenly spaced 4-inch Circles, with a 3½-inch circle in the middle. The longer (side) borders have a 6-inch Circle at each end, then four evenly spaced 4-inch Circles and a 3½-inch Circle in the middle.

10 Use appliqué glue to hold them in position, then sew them in place, following the instructions on page 198.

11 Join the short borders to the top and bottom, and the long borders to the sides. Measure the quilt top through the center in both directions. It should now measure 41 x 43 inches.

BORDER 3 (PATTERNED-STRIPED)

12 Take the four patterned-striped strips for Border 3 and cross cut two strips, 3¼ x 41 inches, for top and bottom borders, and two strips, 3¼ x 43 inches, for the sides.

13 Sew the shorter strips to the top and bottom of the quilt top.

14 Sew a blue-floral rectangle to either end of the remaining strips. Pin, and then sew them to the sides. Measure the quilt top through the center in both directions. It should now measure 46½ x 48½ inches.

Diagram 1

Diagram 2

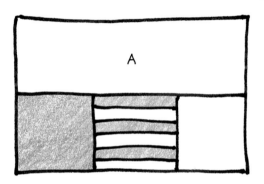
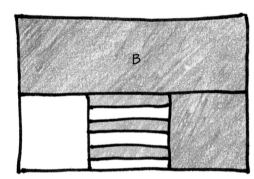

BORDER 4 (PIECED)

15 Take the 54 squares of each of the narrow-striped, light-patterned, and dark-plum fabrics for Border 4, and make 54 units that have a light square and a dark square with a striped square in the middle (Diagram 1). Take the 26 rectangles in each of the light and dark fabrics and sew a rectangle to each of the pieced units (Diagram 2), making 26 sets with a light rectangle on top (A), and 26 with a dark (B). You will have two single three-square units left over.

16 To make the side borders, construct two identical strips of 12 units each, starting with a Unit A and alternating the A and B units (Diagram 3).

17 Using the photograph as a guide as to how the borders are positioned, pin, and then sew a shorter border to either side of the quilt top.

18 To make the top and bottom borders, construct two identical strips of 14 units each, starting with a Unit B, and alternating the A and B units. Using the photograph as a guide and keeping the color sequence correct, sew a single three-square unit to one end of each top and bottom border. Pin, and then sew the borders into place. Measure the quilt top through the center in both directions. It should now measure 58½ x 60½ inches.

Diagram 3

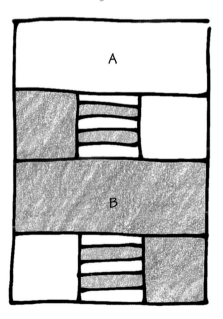

BORDER 5 (DARK PLUM)

19 Take the joined dark-plum strip for Border 5 and cross cut to make two strips, 2½ x 60½ inches, and two strips, 2½ x 58½ inches.

20 Matching centers and ends, pin, and then sew the two shorter trips to the sides of the quilt.

21 Sew a blue-floral corner square to either end of the remaining strips, pin, and then sew them in place. Measure the quilt top through the center in both directions. It should now measure 62½ x 64½ inches.

BORDER 6 (APPLIQUÉD CIRCLES)

22 Take the joined narrow-striped strip for Border 6 and cross cut to make two strips, 2 x 62½ inches, and two strips, 2 x 79½ inches. Take the joined light-patterned strip for Border 6 and cross cut to make four strips, 3½ x 62½ inches, and four strips, 3½ x 79½ inches.

23 Following the piecing details in Step 8, on page 154, sew two sets of pieced borders for the top and bottom and sides of the quilt top.

24 Repeat the appliqué procedure as for Border 3 and sew in place. The top and bottom borders each have three evenly spaced 6-inch Circles, and the side borders have a 7½-inch Circle at each end, as well as three evenly spaced 6-inch Circles.

25 When appliqué is complete, sew the shorter borders to the top and bottom and the longer borders to the sides. Measure the quilt top through the center in both directions. It should now measure 77½ x 79½ inches.

BORDER 7 (PLAID)

26 Take the joined plaid strip for Border 7 and cross cut two strips, 5 x 79½ inches, and two strips, 5 x 86½ inches.

27 Pin, and then sew the two shorter strips to the sides of the quilt. Repeat with the longer strips for top and bottom. Your quilt top is complete!

Backing, quilting, and binding

Cut the backing fabric crosswise into three 92-inch pieces. Remove the selvages and stitch the pieces together. Press the seams open and press the backing piece carefully.

Refer to pages 204–211 for instructions on finishing.

Even though Bluebirds & Happiness has appliqué, I machine-quilted it with a flowing pattern and white cotton. I like the way the quilt goes back and forth from traditional to contemporary influences. And in case you're wondering, I love the plaid border, because it pulls out the oranges from the center medallion gloriously ... and it reminds me of a picnic blanket from which we might listen to the birds chirping.

Looking Back

 Sarah Fielke

THE IDEA

The bird in the center medallion of this quilt is looking back through time to a more traditional quilt. I used a plain quilter's muslin for the background, to convey the feeling of antiquity, and the bird is looking into the past, even though its feathers are made from a much more modern fabric.

Although it looks fiddly, this quilt is actually a good introduction to appliqué. There are lots of leaves, but they are all the same shape and good for practice before you tackle the slightly more difficult shapes of the tail and the reverse appliqué in the border flowers.

I would love to see this quilt done on a dark background with bright, tropical colors. If you make one, be sure to send us a picture!

Finished quilt size
Throw or wall-hanging, 68½ inches square

Materials and tools
2½ yards cream quilter's muslin for background and Triangle Border
6 inches small pink-print fabric for Triangle Border
⅝ yard blue-spotted fabric for Narrow Borders and birds' wings
1½ yards large cream-floral print fabric for Outer Border
¼ yard medium pink/cream-floral fabric for birds and large flowers
⅜ yard pink/cream-geometric fabric for birds, flowers, and tulips
Small piece (4-inch square) teal-blue fabric for feature bird's wing
⅛ yard yellow-and-green-floral fabric for tulips
⅛ yard yellow-striped fabric for tulips
⅛ yard aqua-striped fabric for tops of large flowers
¼ yard cream-patterned fabric for detail on flowers
Fat quarter brown-geometric fabric for stems
½ yard green fabric for leaves
⅔ yard pink fabric for binding
4⅛ yards backing fabric, or 75-inch square
75-inch-square cotton batting
Rotary cutter, quilter's ruler, and cutting mat
Neutral-colored cotton thread for piecing
Appliqué needles and cotton thread to match appliqué fabrics
Template plastic, 2B pencil, and silver gel pen
Short appliqué pins or appliqué glue
Stranded embroidery floss in three different shades of pink
3 balls cream and 1 ball green perle cotton no. 8 for hand-quilting

NOTE: *It is recommended that all fabrics be 100 percent cotton, and be ironed. Requirements are based on fabric 44 inches wide. Unless otherwise stated, all seam allowances are ¼ inch throughout. Color test any dark fabrics that you are using (see page 189), and wash them before cutting if they run.*

Please read all instructions before starting.

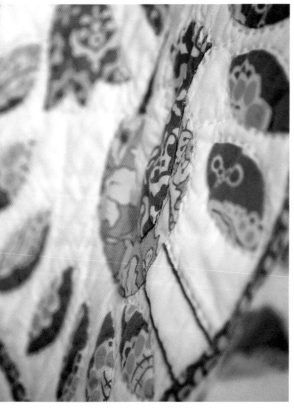

Templates

All appliqué shapes are on the pattern sheet. Trace Leaf A, Bird B, Tulip C, Large Flower D, Wing E, Flower Top F, and Reverse Flower Background G onto template plastic, label them, and cut them out accurately.

Cutting

All fabrics are strip cut across the width of the fabric from fold to selvage unless otherwise specified, or unless you are using a directional print (cut off all selvages first). Cut the largest pieces first.

FROM CREAM QUILTER'S MUSLIN, CUT:

- One strip, 21 inches wide. From this strip, cut one 21-inch square for the appliqué background. (This square is ½ inch too big, to allow for fraying while you work the appliqué, and will eventually be trimmed back to 20½ inches.) From the remaining fabric in this strip, cut 22 squares, each 2⅞ inches. Cross cut these squares into 44 half-square triangles for the Triangle Border. Cut also four squares, each 2½ inches, for the corners of the Triangle Border.
- Four strips, 10½ inches wide, for the Appliqué Border.
- Two strips, 10½ inches wide. Cross cut into eight squares, each 10½ inches, for the Appliqué Border corners and Outer Border corners.

FROM SMALL PINK-PRINT FABRIC, CUT:

- Two strips, 2⅞ inches wide. Cross cut 22 squares, each 2⅞ inches. Cross cut these squares into 44 half-square triangles, for the Triangle Border.

FROM LARGE CREAM-FLORAL FABRIC, CUT:

- Four strips, each 10½ x 56 inches, along the length of the fabric, for Outer Border.

NOTE: *This fabric is cut along the length, not the width, so that it doesn't have to be joined.*

FROM BLUE-SPOTTED FABRIC, CUT:

- Nine strips, 1½ inches wide. Cross cut two of these strips into two strips, each 1½ x 20½ inches, and two strips, each 1½ x 22½ inches, for Narrow Border 1. Stitch the remaining strips together, end to end, to make one long length. Reserve this strip for Narrow Border 2.

APPLIQUÉ FABRICS

The appliqué shapes do not include seam allowance. Please read the appliqué instructions on page 198 carefully before you begin. Trace around the shapes on the right side of the fabric using a silver gel pen or a 2B pencil, then cut the shapes out, leaving a scant ¼ inch seam allowance around each one. When cutting the Large Flower shape D, trace the reverse appliqué detail onto the shape, but do not cut out until Background G is basted behind. I recommend keeping your shapes in a plastic loose-leaf folder so that you can see what you have and they don't get lost or crushed.

FROM GREEN LEAF FABRIC, CUT:
- 59 Leaves, using Template A.

FROM MEDIUM PINK/CREAM-FLORAL FABRIC, CUT:
- Two Birds, using Template B, and one Bird, using the reverse of Template B.
- Two Large Flowers, using Template D.

FROM PINK/CREAM-GEOMETRIC FABRIC, CUT:
- One Bird, using Template B, and one Bird, using the reverse of Template B.
- Four Tulips, using Template C.
- Two Large Flowers, using Template D.

FROM SMALL PIECE OF TEAL-BLUE FABRIC, CUT:
- One Wing, using Template E.

FROM REMAINING BLUE-SPOTTED FABRIC, CUT:
- Four Wings, using Template E.

FROM YELLOW-AND-GREEN-FLORAL FABRIC, CUT:
- Eight Tulips, using Template C.

FROM YELLOW-STRIPED FABRIC, CUT:
- Four Tulips, using Template C.

FROM AQUA-STRIPED FABRIC, CUT:
- Four Flower Tops, using Template F.

FROM CREAM-PATTERNED FABRIC, CUT:
- Four Reverse Flower Backgrounds, using Template G.

FROM BROWN-GEOMETRIC FABRIC:
- Establish a 45-degree angle using your rotary ruler and cut the fabric into 1-inch strips on the bias. You need this amount of fabric to get the right length of bias strip. You may find that joining the strips into one long piece and then cutting the correct size off the long piece is

the easiest method. When you have cut the bias strips, iron them into thirds so you are left with a strip approximately ⅞ inch wide, which will be used for the flower stems.

FROM BINDING FABRIC, CUT:
- Nine strips, 2½ inches wide. Join the strips, end to end, using 45-degree seams, and press seams to one side.

Constructing the quilt top

CENTER APPLIQUÉ PANEL

1 Find the center of the muslin background piece by folding it into quarters and finger-pressing the center. Center the appliqué outline underneath the fabric. Trace the placement of the appliqué pieces lightly onto the muslin background using a 2B pencil or gel pen, including the bird's beak. You may use your favorite method of appliqué to attach the pieces to the background. I used needle-turn appliqué and fabric glue (see page 198).

2 After completing the appliqué, use three strands of embroidery floss, one of each color pink, to satin stitch the bird's beak and eye. Using three different strands gives the embroidery a variegated appearance.

3 When you have completed the appliqué panel, press it carefully, and trim it to 20½ inches square.

NARROW BORDER 1 (BLUE-SPOTTED)

4 Sew two of the 1½ x 20½-inch blue-spotted strips to the top and bottom edges of the center panel.

5 Sew the 1½ x 22½-inch blue-spotted strips to the remaining sides. Press seams away from the center toward the border. The top should now measure 22½ inches square.

TRIANGLE BORDER

6 Take the 44 muslin and 44 pink half-square triangles and sew them into pairs along the diagonal edge to form 44 squares.

7 Using the photograph as a guide for the direction of the triangles, piece four strips of 11 squares each.

8 Sew a 2½-inch muslin square to either end of two of the strips.

9 Find the center of the top edge of the quilt top and mark with a pin. Find the center of one of the shorter triangle borders, match the centers, and pin. Next, match and pin the ends, pin the edges in between, and then sew. Repeat with the bottom edge of the quilt top.

10 Taking care to match the corners, attach the longer borders to either side of the quilt top in the same manner. Press. The top should now measure 26½ inches square.

Diagram 1

Diagram 2

APPLIQUÉ BORDER

(The border must be attached to the quilt before the appliqué is completed, as the design turns the corner.)

11 Measure the length of the quilt top through the center, and then cut the four 10½-inch-wide muslin border strips to that size.

12 Attach a border strip to the top and bottom edges of the quilt top, as for the Triangle Border.

13 Sew a 10½-inch square to both ends of the remaining border strips, and then attach these strips to either side, as before, taking care to match the corners. Press.

14 Complete the reverse appliqué detail (see page 200) on the Large Flowers before you sew them to the background. Baste or glue the cream-floral Background Flower G behind the Large Flower D (Diagram 1), and then carefully snip away the detail outlines on Flower D, leaving a scant ¼-inch seam allowance. Clip curves, finger-press seam allowance under, and stitch the edges in place, to reveal the background fabric beneath (Diagram 2). Carefully trim away any excess background fabric from behind the design. Complete all four Large Flowers in this way.

15 Now appliqué each Large Flower to a Flower Top F, thus completing the flowers.

16 Find the center of the border strips and match it to the center of the appliqué border pattern. Trace the pattern lightly onto the muslin, using a 2B pencil, and complete the appliqué in the same manner as the center panel. The top should now measure 46½ inches square. (If your measurements differ, you will need to adjust the border measurements.)

NARROW BORDER 2 (BLUE-SPOTTED)

17 From the joined strip of border fabric, cut two strips, each 1½ x 46½ inches, and two strips, each 1½ x 48½ inches.

18 Find the center of the top edge of the quilt top and mark with a pin. Find the center of one of the shorter (1½ x 46½-inch) blue-spotted border strips, match the centers, and pin. Next, pin the ends, pin the edges in between, and then sew. Repeat with bottom edge of the quilt top.

19 In the same manner, sew the two longer (1½ x 48½-inch) blue-spotted strips to the remaining sides. Press seams toward the borders. The top should now measure 48½ inches square.

CORNER BLOCK APPLIQUÉ

20 Trace the appliqué pattern (the bird from the center panel) onto the remaining four 10½-inch muslin corner blocks. Complete the border corner appliqué and embroider the bird's beak and eyes as for the Center Appliqué Panel.

OUTER BORDER (CREAM-FLORAL)

21 Measure the quilt top through the center and trim the four large cream-floral border strips to this length.

22 Attach the top and bottom borders, as before, by finding and pinning the centers and ends, pinning in between, and then sewing.

23 Attach an appliquéd corner block to each end of the side border strips, using the photograph as a guide to make sure that the birds face in the correct direction.

24 Pin and sew the borders to the sides of the quilt top, as before, and press. Your quilt top is complete!

Backing, quilting, and binding

If you are using the narrower backing fabric, cut it in half crosswise, giving two 74-inch pieces. Remove the selvages and stitch the pieces together up the middle seam. Press the seam open and press the backing piece carefully.

Refer to pages 204–211 for instructions on finishing.

Looking Back is hand-quilted using cream and green perle cotton no. 8. I outline-quilted all the appliqué shapes and triangles using a light green cotton, and then cross-hatched the backgrounds in cream. I used different widths of masking tape to make the straight lines, so I didn't have to mark the quilt top.

Shared Inspiration

Believe it or not, both of these quilts are based on the exact same template.
We set the challenge to use the template to make a quilt, and look what happened!
The individual star blocks are the same, but settings, borders, and color choices
create completely different quilts. One has a solid border, based on a vertical
repeat fabric, and the other has a strip-pieced border. Both are set using
60-degree angles due to the block finishing as a hexagon.

Jazz Hands

Erica's Honesty

Jazz Hands

 Sarah Fielke

THE IDEA

I started piecing the blocks for this challenge without a lot of thought as to how they would go together. I grabbed some spots, stripes, a few favorites, and away I went. With 72 pieces in each block and many blocks to make, I figured I had a while to sew them, and what a great carry-along project it would be on airplanes or on long car trips. When I suddenly realized I was going to have to finish it for the book, there was a moment of panic until I went with what I know—that another spot or two will always save the day.

When I was naming this project, words kept coming to mind: Buzzy, fizzy, poppy, dotty, and jumpy. But in the end, I came down to Jazz Hands. Can't you see the jazz dancers with their outstretched fingers?

Finished quilt size

Throw, 49 x 61½ inches
Finished block size: 16 inches from point to point of hexagon; 14 inches from point to point of star

Materials and tools

⅛ yard each of 13 different-colored spotted white fabrics for star backgrounds (A)
A large assortment of scraps, or a total of:
   ½ yard striped fabric for star centers (B)
   ⅞ yard fabric for inner border of stars (C)
   ⅞ yard fabric for second border of stars (D)
   ⅞ yard fabric for secondary points of stars (E)
   ½ yard fabric for outer points of stars (F)
(You will need ⅛ yard each of five different star fabrics for each block if you are buying by the yard for this project)
⅞ yard dark blue-spotted fabric for setting
Assorted spotted scraps, or a total of 1⅜ yards spotted fabrics for outer border, or ⅛ yard of 13 different spotted fabrics
¾ yard brown-geometric for binding
3⅞ yards backing fabric
55 x 69 inches cotton batting
Template plastic, 2B pencil, and black permanent marker
Rotary cutter, quilter's ruler, and cutting mat
60-degree ruler (optional) and ¼-inch ruler
Neutral-colored cotton thread for piecing
3 balls dark blue perle cotton no. 8 for hand-quilting

NOTE: *It is recommended that all fabrics be 100 percent cotton, and be ironed. Requirements are based on fabric 44 inches wide. Unless otherwise stated, all seam allowances are ¼ inch throughout. Color test any dark fabrics that you are using (see page 189), and wash them before cutting if they run.*
   Please read all instructions before starting.

Templates

Template 1 and Template 2A are printed on the pattern sheet. Trace Template 1 onto template plastic using a sharp 2B pencil. Mark the line for the ¼-inch seam onto the template plastic with black pen. Color in the ¼-inch seam allowance around the outside edge of the template, using the pen. This gives you a window to enable fussy-cutting of stripes and patterned fabrics when you are tracing around the template.

If you are not using the 60-degree ruler, you also need to trace Template 2A (Half-triangle and Reverse) onto paper to use as a guide under your ruler. Cut the templates out using sharp scissors—not fabric scissors!

Cutting

All fabrics are strip cut across the width of the fabric from fold to selvage unless otherwise specified, or unless you are using a directional print (cut off all selvages first). Cut the largest pieces first. There are 72 pieces in each star block, so try to be as precise as possible when cutting and piecing. However, your finished block may not measure exactly what it should, so measure the quilt top before cutting any border fabrics precisely.

STARS

Each complete star is composed of 72 Template 1 pieces, cut from six different fabrics—a spotted white background fabric and five fabrics for the star itself. The placement of your fabric will determine which section of the star comes forward. Placing a brighter or darker fabric at the star point and a lighter fabric for the secondary point of the star will result in a very definite star shape, and making the outer points more blended and the centers lighter or darker will result in more of a hexagon. It is important that all outer fabrics have good contrast with the background fabric.

To cut each shape, using Template 1 and a very sharp pencil, trace the appropriate number of Template 1 outlines onto the back of each fabric. Using the ¼-inch ruler, mark a ¼-inch seam line onto the shapes (this is your sewing line), and then cut the fabric shapes out, using scissors.

Lay the pieces of the block out on a scrap of batting or in a block book. Arrange the colors until you are happy with the layout and the way the star appears. It is quite difficult to see how the star will appear until you have cut some of the pieces out. If you have cut the pieces and decide the colors are wrong, put them aside and try out others. You can always use the ones you have cut in another color combination for another block.

There are many different little pieces in these blocks. Put all the pieces for each block into a separate plastic ziplock bag, to keep everything together.

You will need 11 complete stars and two half-stars. Cut each star as follows (halving the number of pieces for the two half-stars):

FROM SPOTTED WHITE BACKGROUND FABRIC (A), CUT:

- 24 Template 1 pieces.

FROM STRIPED STAR CENTER FABRIC (B), CUT:

- Six Template 1 pieces.

FROM THE FIRST BORDER FABRIC (C), CUT:

- 12 Template 1 pieces.

FROM THE SECOND BORDER FABRIC (D), CUT:

- 12 Template 1 pieces.

FROM THE SECONDARY POINT FABRIC (E), CUT:

- 12 Template 1 pieces.

FROM THE STAR POINT FABRIC (F), CUT:

- Six Template 1 pieces.

FROM BLUE-SPOTTED SETTING FABRIC, CUT:

- Four strips, 2 inches wide. Cross cut into 16 strips, each 2 x 10½ inches, for the zigzag setting strips.
- Two strips, 7½ inches wide, for setting triangles. Using the 60-degree ruler or Template 2A, cross cut these strips into 16 triangles (flip the template or ruler to give eight 2A and eight 2A Reverse triangles.)
- One strip, 3 inches wide. Cross cut this strip into four squares, each 3 inches, for the border corners.

FROM EACH OF THE SPOTTED OUTER BORDER FABRICS, CUT:

- One strip, 3 inches wide. Cross cut these strips into random lengths of 1½, 2, and 2½ inches across the width.

FROM BINDING FABRIC, CUT:

- Bias strips, 2½ inches wide, with a total sewn length of 6¾ yards, using the 45-degree angle on your quilter's ruler. (If you are not having rounded corners on your quilt, you can cut straight binding instead of bias.) Join the strips, end to end, using 45-degree seams, and press seams to one side.

Diagram 1

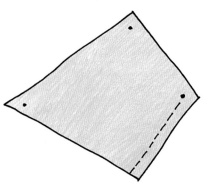

Diagram 2

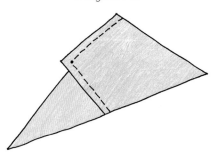

Diagram 3

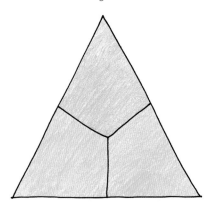

Constructing the quilt top

STAR BLOCKS (MAKE 11 + 2 HALF-STARS)

1   Lay out the pieces of each star block in order, ready to sew. The star is composed of twenty-four 60-degree triangle units, each of which, in turn, is composed of three Template 1 pieces (see Star Block Assembly diagram).

2   Referring to the instructions for hand-piecing (see page 196), and the Star Block Assembly diagram, sew two Template 1 pieces together along one shorter edge, starting at the outside edge, and stopping at the marked dot at the end of the seam line (Diagram 1).

3   Pin a third Template 1 piece to the pieced unit, folding one section out of the way. Stitch from the outside edge to the marked center dot, as before (Diagram 2).

4   Repeat on the remaining short edge to complete one 60-degree triangle unit (Diagram 3). Press.

5   Continue to piece each 60-degree triangle unit together in this manner, laying the pieces out as you go to avoid confusion. You will need six Star Center units, 12 Background units, and six Star Point units (Diagram 4).

6   When you have pieced the 24 triangle units, sew a Star Center unit to a Star Point unit, and then sew a Background unit to each side of this and press carefully (Diagram 5). At this point, it is important to pay attention to which way the seams are pressed in your blocks. Pressing the seam toward the star center and the star points, and away from the secondary star points, will result in the centers and the points being

Star Block Assembly

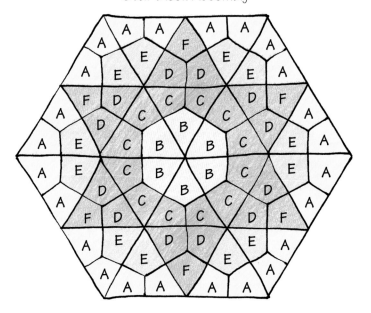

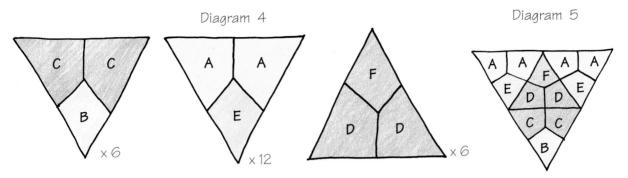

Diagram 4

Diagram 5

a feature and the background receding. It will also result in a flat and cleanly pieced block.

7 Next, piece three of the larger triangles you have created into a half-star unit, stopping sewing at the marked dot on each seam at the center of the star, as before (Diagram 6).

8 Repeat to make 22 half-star units plus two extra half-stars (24 half-stars in all). Each of these half-stars contains 36 pieces—lots of room for error! Try to be as accurate as possible, so that all your half-stars turn out the same size. They should measure 7½ inches from the flat side to the middle, including seam allowance. If you consistently get a different size, you will need to adjust the size of your setting triangles. You will eventually make 11 whole stars and two half-stars; however, do not piece the whole stars together across the middle yet, but rather, leave them in halves for easier assembly of the quilt top later on.

ADDING SETTING TRIANGLES AND STRIPS

9 When you have pieced all 24 half-star units, lay them out, according to the quilt photograph, on the floor or on a design wall, and move them around until you are happy with the placement and color balance.

10 For the first row, sew a setting half-triangle to one side of a half-star, and then sew a 2 x 10½-inch strip to the other side, followed by another half-star, another strip, a third half-star, and finally, another setting triangle of the opposite orientation to finish (Diagram 7). Note that the setting strips are too large for the blocks! When you begin

Diagram 6

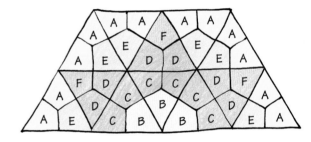

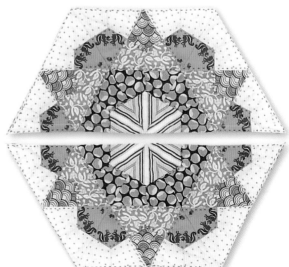

Diagram 7

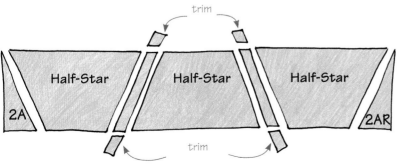

sewing them to the block, leave 1 inch above the top of the block, and you will end up with 1 inch below the end of the block. When you have sewn the row together, use your straight quilter's ruler to trim off the strips so that the row is straight.

11 Repeat with the remaining rows until you have pieced the quilt top into eight rows. Taking care to pin the points for accuracy, sew the rows together across the width of the quilt until you have completed all eight rows. The center of the quilt is now complete and should measure 44 x 56½ inches. (If your measurements differ because of all the piecing, you will need to adapt the border measurements.) Press.

OUTER BORDER

12 Take all the pieces of 3-inch-wide spotted fabric and sew them randomly, end to end, along the 3-inch edge into a long strip measuring at least 5½ yards. Press all the seams to one side. From this strip, cut two pieces, each 44 x 3 inches, and two pieces, each 56½ x 3 inches.

13 Find the center of one of the shorter strips and the center of the top of the quilt and pin. Pin the ends, and then pin the edges in between, easing as you pin. Sew and repeat with the bottom of the quilt. Press.

14 Sew a blue-spotted 3-inch square to either end of the remaining border strips. Using the same process, sew the strips to either side of the quilt top. Press.

15 Using an upturned saucer or similar, make a template of the corner curve and lay the template on the corners of the quilt. Using a rotary cutter, trim the corners of the quilt into neat curves. Your quilt top is complete!

Backing, quilting, and binding

Cut the backing fabric crosswise in half into two 69½-inch pieces. Remove the selvages and stitch the pieces together up the middle seam. Press the seam allowance open and press the backing piece carefully.

Refer to pages 204–211 for instructions on finishing.

Jazz Hands was hand-quilted with perle cotton no. 8 in dark blue, to match the setting triangles. I outline-quilted around the pieces in the star on the low side of the seams. I then cross-hatched the setting triangles, using 1-inch masking tape as a guide.

Bind the quilt following the instructions on page 210, but instead of folding the corners into miters, when you reach the curved corner, use the bias in the binding to curve around the corner as you stitch. Take care not to pull the fabric or the corners will pucker when the quilt is flat. Finish as for straight binding.

Erica's Honesty

 Kathy Doughty

THE IDEA

Let's be honest, when someone asks for an opinion on a work in progress, it's sometimes hard to be truthful. In this case, I had hand-pieced and joined the blocks, but there was something not quite right. When I asked, everyone said how nice it was. But Erica gently made me see that a few blocks weren't set in perfectly, and that, well, the setting fabric wasn't interesting enough. Hmm . . . in an instant, I knew she was right and set out immediately to unpick and remake the entire quilt. I thank her here for a brave and honest friendship by naming the quilt after her.

The border utilizes vertical prints. When you see gorgeous vertical prints, buy them for the length of the quilt plus the width of the top and border. They are a stunning finish to a quilt!

Finished quilt size

Single, 68½ x 76½ inches

Finished block size: 16 inches from point to point of hexagon; 14 inches from point to point of star

Materials and tools

1¾ yards directional-print fabric, or 1⅔ yards non-directional fabric, for Outer Border

½ yard dark-spotted fabric for Inner Border

⅓ yard print fabric for Corner Squares

1¾ yards fabric for star background (A)

A large assortment of scraps, or a total of:

    ½ yard fabric for centers of stars (B)

    ⅞ yard fabric for inner border of stars (C)

    ⅞ yard fabric for second border of stars (D)

    ⅞ yard fabric for secondary points of stars (E)

    ½ yard fabric for outer points of stars (F)

¾ yard yellow-checked fabric for setting triangles/diamonds

⅔ yard binding fabric

83-inch-square wool batting

4⅝ yards backing fabric

Template plastic, 2B pencil, and black permanent pen

60-degree ruler (optional) and ¼-inch ruler

Rotary cutter, quilter's ruler, and cutting mat

Neutral-colored cotton thread for piecing

3 balls perle cotton no. 8, in colors to match fabrics, for quilting

DESIGN TIP: *Each star has a dark fabric for the outer point, and they generally have one inspiration fabric that sets the palette for the rest of the sections. The setting fabric has a bit of graphic energy to slightly blend between the stars. The border fabric has a screen-printed design that runs the length of the quilt. The inner border and the binding are strong, like the star points, to contain the quilt and finish it off.*

NOTE: *It is recommended that all fabrics be 100 percent cotton, and be ironed. Requirements are based on fabric 44 inches wide. Unless otherwise stated, all seam allowances are ¼ inch throughout. Color test any dark fabrics that you are using (see page 189), and wash them before cutting if they run.*

Please read all instructions before starting.

Templates

Templates 1, 2A, and 3B are printed on the pattern sheet. Trace Template 1 onto template plastic using a sharp 2B pencil. If you are not using the 60-degree ruler, you also need to trace Template 2A (Half-triangle and Reverse) and Template 3B (Full Triangle) onto paper, as well as create the full Diamond (D) and Half-diamond (C) to use as guides with your quilter's ruler. To obtain the Diamond template, trace a complete Template 3B onto paper, then flip it over along the fold line (the seam line) and trace a mirror image for the remaining half of the diamond. To obtain the Half-diamond, trace a Template 2A Half-triangle onto paper, then flip it over along the fold line (the seam line) and trace a mirror image for the remaining half of the half-diamond. Cut the plastic and paper templates out using sharp scissors—not fabric scissors! Mark the dots and the line for the ¼-inch seam onto the template plastic with the black permanent pen.

Cutting

All fabrics are strip cut across the width of the fabric from fold to selvage, unless otherwise specified, or unless you are using a directional print (cut off all selvages first). Cut the largest pieces first.

STARS

Each complete star is composed of 72 Template 1 pieces, cut from six different fabrics—a background fabric and five fabrics for the star itself. Ensure that all outer fabrics have good contrast with the background fabric.

Using Template 1 and a very sharp pencil, trace the appropriate number of Template 1 outlines onto the back of each fabric. Using the ¼-inch ruler, mark the ¼-inch seam line onto the shapes (this is your sewing line), and then cut the fabric shapes out, using scissors.

Lay the pieces of the block out on a scrap of batting or in a block book. Arrange the colors until you are happy with the layout. It is quite difficult to see how the star will appear until you have cut some of the pieces out. If the colors are wrong, put them aside and try out others. You can always use the ones you have cut in another color combination for another block.

Put all the pieces for each block into a separate plastic ziplock bag. You will need 12 complete stars. Cut each star as follows:

FROM STAR BACKGROUND FABRIC (A), CUT:
- 24 Template 1 pieces.

FROM STAR CENTER FABRIC (B), CUT:
- Six Template 1 pieces.

FROM THE FIRST BORDER FABRIC (C), CUT:
- 12 Template 1 pieces.

FROM THE SECOND BORDER FABRIC (D), CUT:
- 12 Template 1 pieces.

FROM THE SECONDARY POINT FABRIC (E), CUT:
- 12 Template 1 pieces.

FROM THE STAR POINT FABRIC (F), CUT:
- Six Template 1 pieces.

FROM DARK-SPOTTED FABRIC, CUT:
- Seven strips, 2 inches wide. Join them end to end and set aside for the Inner Borders.

FROM DIRECTIONAL-PRINT OUTER BORDER FABRIC, CUT:
- Two strips, 9 inches wide, along the length of the fabric, and set aside for the side Outer Borders.
- Five strips, 9 inches wide, across the remaining width. Join them together, end to end, keeping the pattern correct, and set aside for the top and bottom Outer Borders.

OR, FROM NON-DIRECTIONAL OUTER BORDER FABRIC, CUT:
- Six strips, 9 inches wide. Join them together end to end and set aside for the Outer Borders.

FROM CORNER SQUARE FABRIC, CUT:
- One strip, 9 inches wide. Cross cut to make four squares, each 9 inches.

FROM YELLOW-CHECKED FABRIC, CUT:
- Two strips, 7½ inches wide. Using either the 60-degree ruler or the paper Diamond template under your straight-edged quilter's ruler, cross cut six diamonds (see Cutting Diagram, page 180).

Cutting Diagram

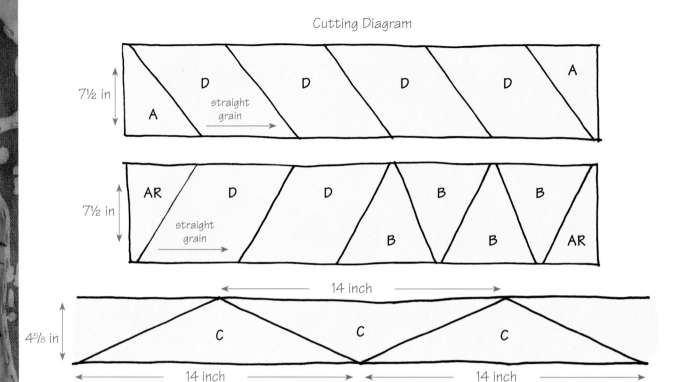

7½ in

A   D   straight grain   D   D   D   A

7½ in

AR   D   straight grain   D   B   B   B   B   AR

4⅝ in

14 inch

C   C   C

14 inch   14 inch

- Use the remaining scraps from the diamonds to cut four half-triangles (two 2A and two 2A Reverse) for the corners, and four setting triangles (Template 3B) for the top and bottom edges.
- Two strips, 4⅝ inches wide. Cross cut six half-diamond shapes, using the paper Half-diamond Template as a guide.

FROM BINDING FABRIC, CUT:

- Nine strips, 2½ inches wide. Join the strips, end to end, using 45-degree seams, and press seams to one side.

Constructing the quilt top

STAR BLOCKS (MAKE 12)

Follow Steps 1 to 7 of Jazz Hands, on pages 172–173.

8   Make 12 pairs of half-star units (24 half-stars in all). Each half-star contains 36 pieces—lots of room for error! Try to be as accurate as possible, so that all your half-stars turn out the same size. They should measure 7½ inches from the flat side to the middle, including seam allowance. If you consistently get a different size, you will need to adjust the size of your setting triangles and diamonds. You will eventually make 12 whole stars, each of a different fabric combination, however do not piece the whole stars together across the middle yet. Leave them in halves for easier assembly of the quilt top later on.

9   When you have pieced all 24 half-star units, lay them out, according to the quilt photograph, on the floor or on a design wall, and move them around until you are happy with the placement and color balance of the stars.

10 Now you can begin to assemble the rows. It is easiest to do this on the diagonal, so that you avoid having to set in the diamonds. Following the Quilt Assembly Diagram, lay out and sew the rows diagonally as follows, starting from the upper right-hand corner:

Row 1: Half-triangle corner (A).

Row 2: Half-star 1a, half-diamond (C).

Row 3: Setting triangle (B), half-star 1b, half-star 2a, half-diamond (C).

Row 4: Half-star 3a, diamond (D), half-star 2b, half-star 4a, half-diamond (C).

Row 5: Setting triangle (B), half-star 3b, half-star 5a, diamond (D), half-star 4b, half-star 6a, half-triangle corner (A Reversed).

Row 6: Half-star 7a, diamond (D), half-star 5b, half-star 8a, diamond (D), half-star 6b.

Row 7: Half-triangle corner (A Reversed), half-star 7b, half-star 9a, diamond (D), half-star 8b, half-star 10a, setting triangle (B).

Row 8: Half-diamond (C), half-star 9b, half-star 11a, diamond (D), half-star 10b.

Row 9: Half-diamond (C), half-star 11b, half-star 12a, setting triangle (B).

Row 10: Half-diamond (C), half-star 12b.

Row 11: Half-triangle corner (A).

11 When you have assembled all the rows, sew them together diagonally, one after another, taking care to match points and seam lines. Measure the quilt top through the middle horizontally and vertically. It should now measure 48½ x 56½ inches. (If your measurements differ, you will need to adapt the Inner Border measurements.) Press.

INNER BORDER

12 Trim Inner Border strip to make two strips, 2 x 56½ inches (for sides), two strips, 2 x 51½ inches (for top and bottom), and four strips, each 2 x 9 inches. (Reserve the 9-inch strips for the Outer Border.)

13 Find the middle of the strips and the middle of the side edge of the quilt top, pin, and then sew the longer Inner Border strips to either side of the quilt top.

14 Attach the remaining Inner Border strips to the top and bottom of the quilt top in the same way. Measure the quilt top

Quilt Assembly Diagram

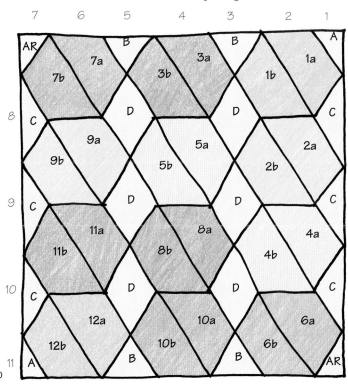

through the center in both directions. It should now measure 51½ x 59½ inches. (If your measurements differ, you will need to adapt the Outer Border measurements accordingly.)

OUTER BORDER

15 Trim the joined Outer Border strip to give a top and bottom Outer Border, each 9 x 48½ inches. Trim the two strips along the length to give two side Outer Border strips, each 9 x 56½ inches.

16 Sew a reserved 2 x 9-inch strip to each end of the top and bottom Outer Border strips.

17 Match the middles and ends and sew the top and bottom Outer Borders to the quilt top.

18 Sew two remaining 2 x 9-inch strips to each end of side Outer Border strips. Sew a 9-inch square to each end of these side border strips.

19 Match the middles and ends of the extended Outer Borders to the quilt top and sew them to the body of the quilt. Your quilt top is complete!

Backing, quilting, and binding

Cut the backing fabric crosswise in half into two 83-inch pieces. Remove the selvages and sew the lengths together to form one backing piece. Press the seams open.

Refer to pages 204–211 for instructions on finishing.

Erica's Honesty is hand-quilted with three colors of perle cotton no. 8 to match the various sections of the quilt. The stars are stabilized with echo-quilting. The diamonds are outline-quilted and also quilted in the middle with a hexagon shape that mirrors the center of the stars. The outside border is where we have some fun, following the lines in the pattern of the fabric around the birds and flowers!

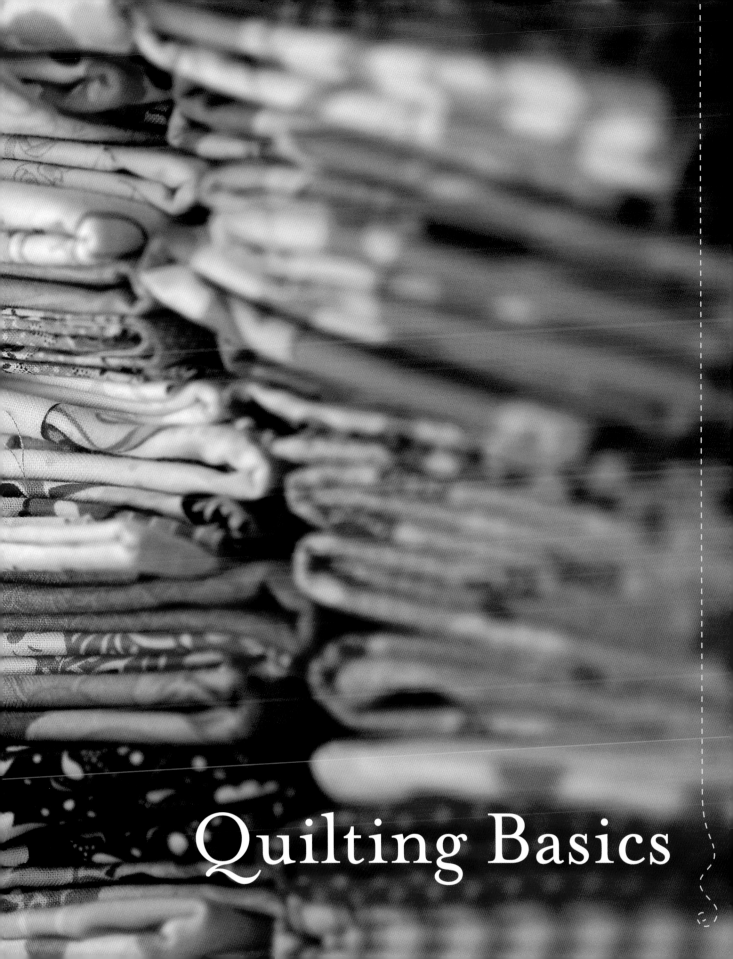

Quilting Basics

FABRIC FOR QUILTS

Selecting fabric is the fun part of making a quilt. We generally use 100 percent cotton fabrics, but also linen blends and some decorator weight fabrics. The important part is that you just love the fabrics and that they work well together.

Fabric can be solid (a uniform color, without a print or pattern), printed, tone-on-tone (having a background printed with a design of the same color), or checked. Printed fabrics may have small, medium, large, or directional prints. Small prints may look almost like solid fabrics from a distance. Medium prints are more distinct and are often used to add visual texture. Large prints have very distinct patterns that stand out from the background, and are often used in quilts as borders or feature prints. Directional prints have a very distinct pattern that runs in one direction on the fabric. They can be particularly effective when used in a border or in a strippy quilt.

When choosing fabrics, think about both the balance of prints and plains as well as the tonal values of the fabrics, that is, the mixture of light, medium, and dark fabrics. You will also find that the effect of a fabric may change according to the various values of the other fabrics surrounding it, often with surprising results. Experimenting with color, tone, and pattern is one of the pleasures of quilting.

FABRIC GRAIN

Fabric has three grains. The lengthwise grain runs the length of the fabric, from top to bottom. The cross grain runs the width of the fabric, from selvage to selvage. Both the lengthwise and cross grains are straight grains. The bias grain runs at a 45-degree angle to the straight grain.

When cutting fabrics, most instructions and templates will tell you to cut on the straight of the grain. Rotary-cut strips are usually cut on the cross grain. An arrow on the template or pattern piece shows you the direction in which the grain should run when cutting out the fabric.

Cutting fabric on the bias will cause the cut edges to stretch; this is undesirable when piecing, although sometimes unavoidable (as when working with triangles). Where bias occurs, it is important to contain it within the quilt rather than having it along the outer edges, as it is difficult to achieve a neat finish when applying borders and bindings to wavy, bias-cut edges. However, bias can be useful if you need to make the fabric curve, such as when making bindings for a quilt with a curved border, or when making bias strips for curved sections of appliqué.

CHOOSING THREADS

Match the thread to the fabric when piecing; for example, when using cotton fabric, use cotton thread. Avoid using polyester thread with a cotton fabric; over time it will cut through the fibers of the cotton. In most situations, cream, white, or gray threads are appropriate for piecing. If using a multicolored fabric, use a neutral thread, such as gray or beige, to match the tone of the background.

The same rule applies when choosing thread for machine-quilting. Monofilament thread, which is transparent, is the most appropriate thread for machine-quilting quilt tops, as it takes on the color of any fabric with which it is used. Although made of nylon, monofilament thread has the elastic quality of cotton.

Monofilament thread should be used as the top thread in the machine. In the bobbin, use a quilting thread that matches the backing fabric. The top tension in the machine should be eased off so that the heavier quilting thread will anchor the quilting stitches in the batting.

When machine-piecing, use a stitch length of about 2.5 to produce 12–14 stitches per inch.

ROTARY CUTTER SAFETY HINTS

Safety should be a priority when using the rotary cutter. The blade should be exposed only when a cut is to be made, and the protective sheath should be replaced as soon as the cut is finished, to protect you and to prevent the blade from being damaged.

Never leave rotary cutters lying about where they can be found by children or pets.

A rotary cutter is essentially a circular razor blade, so treat it accordingly.

Above: *Warm colors are the ones that remind us of the sun—red, yellow, orange.*

Below: *Cool colors include the blues and greens—think of the sea or a shady tree!*

WORKING WITH COLOR

Contrast is very important in quilts. The art of making fabrics stand out against each other is critical in creating quilts that have both excitement and pizzazz.

In the "old" days, we worked contrast in strictly light, medium, and dark categories. Every block was broken down in this manner.

Today, we have so many wonderful colors and wild-patterned fabrics that it isn't always easy to say which one is "lighter" than the other. Half-closing your eyes and squinting at a fabric can help, but it can still be confusing. One way we have learned to achieve success in this area is to separate the colors into warm and cool categories. Warm colors are easily defined as those that remind us of the sun: yellow, red, and orange. Cool colors are those that bring the sea to mind: blue, green, and purple.

We have to learn to think laterally with colors, to move sideways on the color wheel, while still staying within range. A color wheel is a handy tool. We wouldn't recommend that it is used for every fabric choice, but it is handy when a quilt looks dull. Complementary colors—those that sit opposite each other on the wheel—create the most contrast. The colors that sit next to each other are blends of at least two primary colors, and these colors bleed into each other, moving gradually from one shade to another. The gradual change can be used to great effect as well, but contrast is the life of the quilt.

There is nothing worse than spending a lot of time piecing or appliquéing a block, only to find that it blends into the background without creating an effect. So, when a quilt is looking lackluster, consult the color wheel. It may be that most of the quilt shades sit on one side of the wheel. If you simply add a dash of color from the opposite side, you will immediately find the quilt comes to life!

Most successful projects fall into two tri-color categories: the primaries, which are red, blue, and yellow, or the secondary colors, which are green, purple, and orange. It is interesting to note that most of us find our "comfort zone" in one of these groups. In the shop, we often laugh at a stack of chosen fabric that just happens to match an outfit that the customer might be wearing on that day. It is natural to feel comfortable selecting fabrics that we are familiar with for projects. But if, for some reason, this comfy area becomes a bit dull, try spicing it up by moving up or down the color on the wheel, or even, if you dare, slightly to the right or left! We often find that a tight color program at the start can grow into something more interesting by expanding the color definition a bit, so try working outside your zone every once in a while for an exciting change.

When starting a project, think about the colors you want to use. Separate them into piles by color and then by value. By value, we mean the lightness and darkness of the color. Value still plays a part when using clean colors.

It is important to use the full spectrum of the color. For example, when using red, try including pink through magenta.

Value plays an important part in developing energy in the quilt as well. Graphics also play an important role. When you look through the book, you'll find backgrounds with patterns. In traditional-style quilts, most backgrounds are quilter's muslin, or a mild color, or maybe a shirting fabric. We often substitute patterned fabrics for plains. The graphic energy keeps the eye moving around the quilt, entertained at each point. Things to keep in mind when selecting a background that won't overpower the patterns are simple. Evenly repeating spots blend to backgrounds better than uneven spots or dots. Smaller, evenly repeating stripes do the same. It is good to have elements of color in the background that link to the piecing or appliqué, but don't overpower it. This is a stage in selecting fabric that takes time.

Let the idea settle . . . stand back and have a good look while squinting or, if possible, looking through the camera. It is also best to look straight at the work on a design wall to keep the perspective correct.

Experiment with a few options, but if you find one you like, GO FOR IT!

PREPARING FABRICS

Many quilters prefer to wash, dry, and iron cotton quilt fabrics before use. Wash each fabric separately in warm water with a scrap of white cotton fabric to test if the color runs. If it does, the fabric should be discarded or used for another purpose. Otherwise, when the quilt is washed, the color may run and ruin the quilt.

Washing pre-shrinks fabric and removes all finishes added by the manufacturer. Such finishes can make the fabric stiffer and easier to sew; if you wish to restore the stiffness, spray the fabric lightly with spray starch before sewing.

Before sewing, remove the tightly woven edges (selvages) from all fabrics. These edges shrink at a different rate from the rest of the fabric, so if they are left on and included in seams, they may cause the fabric to pucker and bunch when it is laundered, spoiling all your hard work.

Left: A color wheel indicates the shades that are near each other in value as well as those that are exactly opposite (complementary) in the spectrum.

RULERS

USING A STANDARD QUILTER'S RULER

Rotary-cutting rulers (sometimes called quilter's rulers) are made of transparent acrylic and are designed to be used in conjunction with rotary cutters and mats. It is handy to have two rulers of the same size to assist in cutting strips without having to turn the cutting mat around.

Always measure and cut using the lines on the ruler rather than those on the cutting mat; if you cut too many times along the same lines on the mat, you will both damage the mat and eventually erase or blur the lines, making them inaccurate.

Square rulers, which come in various sizes, are handy but not essential. The larger sizes make it possible to cut large squares in one movement. The smaller square rulers are good for cutting small pieces of fabric and for trimming up.

To cut half-square triangles from a strip, using a standard quilter's ruler, calculate the finished size of the block required and add a ⅞-inch seam allowance. Cut strips and then squares to this measurement. Cut once on the diagonal from corner to corner. Each square will yield two triangles.

To cut quarter-square triangles from a strip, using a standard quilter's ruler, calculate the finished size of the block required and add a 1¼-inch seam allowance. Cut strips and then squares to this measurement. Cut twice on the diagonal from corner to corner. Each square will yield four triangles, with the straight grain edge opposite the right angle.

USING SPECIALIZED RULERS

Quilters of today have wonderful resources available to them to help make quilts that are gorgeous and accurate. We have wonderful fabrics with huge, colorful images, a huge variety of spots and stripes, all-over prints

Above, top: Cross cutting a square along one diagonal gives two half-square triangles.
Above: To make quarter-square triangles, leave the half-square triangles undisturbed on the cutting mat and cut across the second diagonal.
Right: Using the very versatile Kaleido-Ruler to cut the triangles for Stashbuster (page 102).
Far right: The same Kaleido-Ruler can then be turned to cut the half-square triangles needed for the Stashbuster block.

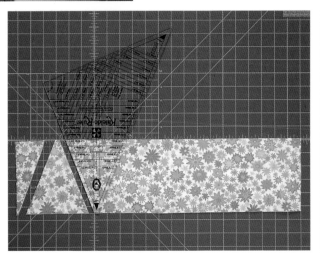

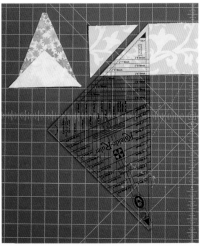

that create energy, and wonderful strong graphics. The combination of these fabrics in the right balance creates a new world of quilting. We are also lucky to have tools that make cutting these fabrics easy and accurate. In this book, we often refer to rulers. These are specially made rulers that take the math and guesswork out of everything, from a half-square triangle to a Dresden Plate wedge. They are generally made from acrylic and can easily be used with a rotary cutter to get the exact shape needed.

There are also acrylic ruler sets that cut out all the shapes needed to make a block. These sets keep the cut shapes a consistent size and allow you to cut more than one at a time. Rulers often have a specific purpose, but if you start to use them, other uses may appear, creating new approaches and new patterns. We encourage you to take a look at the rulers available to you in quilting shops and try them out. All the patterns in the book (except Brighton Rock) have templates or measurements for traditional methods as well as suggestions for rulers—but do try the suggested ruler (or any brand equivalent) and see where it takes you.

HALF-SQUARE AND QUARTER-SQUARE RULERS

Specialized rulers can be used to cut either half-square or quarter-square triangles. These rulers have done the mathematics for you. Simply cut strips as you would for squares. Some rulers have blunt points that allow for the seam allowance at the point of the triangle, eliminating "ears." Calculate the finished size of the triangle required and add ½ inch for the seam allowance. Cut strips to this measurement and establish a straight edge.

To cut half-square triangles, align the ¼-inch mark at the narrow end of the half-square ruler with the top of the cut edge of the strip. Align the edge of the ruler with the cut end of the strip and the blunt point at the top, ensuring that the measurement markings line up flush with the bottom of the strip. Cut the first triangle along the diagonal edge of the ruler. Flip

CUTTING TRIANGLES

It is generally better to sew along the straight grain of a cut piece, as this prevents stretching, which can happen if you sew along a bias edge. Keep this in mind when you are cutting triangles. Half-square triangles have the straight of the grain along their two right-angled sides.

Quarter-square triangles have the straight of the grain along the hypotenuse.

Below, left: If your half-square ruler does not have blunt points, you can simply position the strip ¼ inch below the ruler point, as shown, and you will achieve the same effect.

Below: With a specialized kite-shaped ruler you can cut precise shapes for quilts such as Pop Stars (page 118).

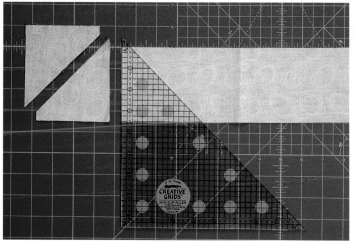

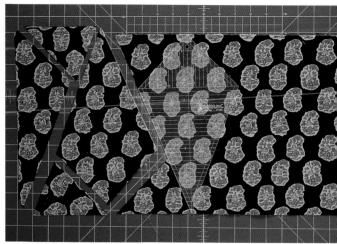

QUARTER-SQUARE TRIANGLES

Align the blunt point of the ruler with the upper cut edge of the fabric and cut along both diagonal edges of the ruler. Flip the ruler so that its blunt point now aligns with the bottom cut edge of the fabric, and the left edge of the ruler with the left cut edge of the fabric strip. Cut along the right diagonal edge of the ruler to create the second triangle.

Diagram 1
Shapes made using a 60-degree ruler

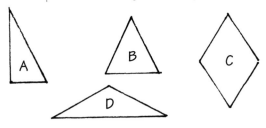

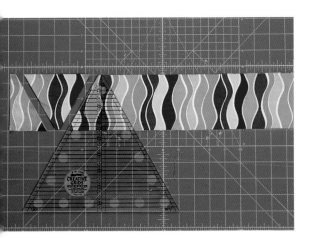

Above: Cutting 60-degree triangles with a 60-degree ruler. The blunt point allows for seam allowance and eliminates "ears."

the ruler, this time placing it so that the ¼-inch mark at the narrow end of the ruler aligns with the lower cut edge of the strip. Cut the second triangle along the straight edge of the ruler. Repeat along the length of the strip.

60-DEGREE RULERS

Using a specialized 60-degree ruler makes it easy to cut a variety of shapes (see Diagram 1), such as diamonds (Shape C), half-diamonds (Shape D), 60-degree triangles (Shape B), and half-triangles (Shape A). Some or all of these shapes are used in several of the quilts in this book, including Brighton Rock (page 12), Jazz Hands (page 168), and Erica's Honesty (page 176). Cutting shapes in this way saves time, increases accuracy, and makes economical use of the fabrics.

The following diagrams show various cutting layouts from strips and the number of each shape that can be produced in each case. The diagrams and instructions here are for shapes cut from an 8½-inch-wide strip cut across the width of the fabric. To determine fabric requirements for other sizes, measure the width of the shape at the base, add the width of the blunt edge, and divide the width of the fabric by this amount.

Be mindful, when cutting A and D shapes, that the cutting line is to the left or right of center on the ruler so as to allow for the seam allowance. The center line is the sewing line in both cases.

CUTTING TRIANGLES AND HALF-TRIANGLES

First, cut a strip ½ inch wider than the finished size of the shape; for example, if you want an 8-inch triangle, cut strips 8½ inches wide. More than one fabric can be cut at once. Now cross cut the strips using the 60-degree ruler. In the illustrated example (Diagram 2), the first and last cuts will yield two half-triangles (A and A Reversed). Flip the ruler to cut the B triangles from the middle of the strip, as shown.

CUTTING DIAMONDS AND HALF-DIAMONDS

As shown in Diagram 3, establish a straight edge at the right end. Unfold to a single layer. Starting at the left end of the strip, place the ruler with the base at the top of the strip, the point at the bottom, and the far left dotted line on the straight edge of the fabric. Cut along the diagonal. This cut will give a half-triangle (Shape A).

Measure 10⅛ inches from the left bottom to the right, mark with a pencil, and do the same for the top. Using the 60-degree ruler (or the 60-degree line on your straight ruler), cut a diagonal line between the points. Repeat twice to create three diamonds (Shape C). When these are cut, fold them in half with the fold at the widest point. Use the ruler to trim to the exact shape, with the 8¼-inch line resting on the fold of the diamond. The remaining fabric in this strip will yield a triangle (Shape B) and a second half-triangle (Shape AR) at the end.

To cut half-diamonds to match the full diamonds, cut a strip 5¼ inches wide, as shown in Diagram 4. Establish a straight edge on both ends of the strip. Using a previously cut half-triangle (Shape A) as a guide, cut along the diagonal from the right end of the strip. Cut away the half-triangle and fold the pointed end until the ruler fits to cut a half-diamond (Shape D). The dotted line to the left of the center on the ruler will line up with the bottom of the strip, and the 8¼-inch line will line up with the folded end. Cut along the diagonal and repeat until there are four half-diamonds. End with a half-triangle (Shape A).

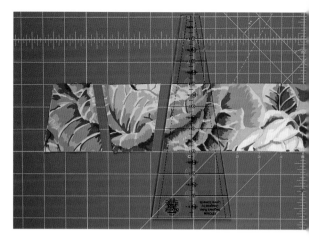

Above: *A wedge ruler makes it easy to cut wedges of any size.*

Diagram 2
Cutting triangles and half-triangles from strips

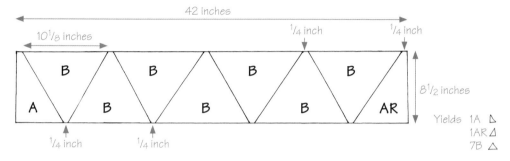

Diagram 3
Cutting diamonds, triangles, and half-triangles from strips

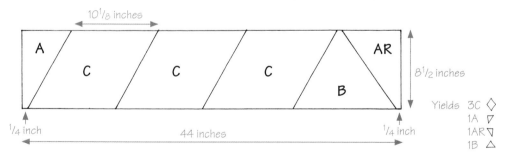

Diagram 4
Cutting half-diamonds and half-triangles from strips

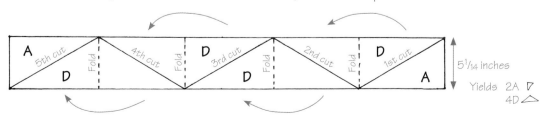

TEMPLATES & TEMPLATE PLASTIC

Transparent template plastic is used to trace shapes onto fabric in much the same way as card stock templates. The advantage of template plastic is that it is much more durable than cardboard, so it can be drawn around numerous times without the shape becoming distorted. It comes in plain and grid versions.

To use template plastic to create a fabric shape, trace the template onto the plastic using a pencil, and then cut it out with a craft knife or paper scissors.

Commercial templates, made of rigid plastic, are also available. They come in various shapes and sizes. They are durable, so they can be used over and over again, and are very precisely cut to give greater accuracy when cutting.

Right: Commercially produced templates come in a great range of shapes and sizes. With accurate seam allowance and point markings, they make cutting specialized shapes, such as this template for Jazz Hands (page 168) and Erica's Honesty (page 176), much more precise.

CUTTING SHAPES BY HAND

Shapes can be cut by hand, using plastic or card stock templates. This method is the most practical for curved shapes. When cutting fabric using templates, the template is generally made to its finished size, that is, without seam allowances; these are added when cutting the fabric. Commercially produced plastic templates are available in various shapes and sizes (often with seam allowance included), or you can make your own templates from thin card or template plastic (from craft stores).

If using templates provided in a magazine or book, photocopy the template, paste it onto thin card stock, and cut it out. Always check the template's dimensions for accuracy and adjust if need be before using it to cut fabric.

Place the template on the wrong side of the fabric and trace around it. (Placing the fabric facedown onto a sheet of fine sandpaper first will prevent it from slipping about on the work surface when you trace around the template.) Use a sharp pencil or fine marker to give the finest line and thus the most accurate seam. This tracing line will become the seam line. Trace the required number of shapes, remembering to allow enough space between them for the seam allowance.

Cut out the shape, allowing a seam allowance of ¼ inch. Most of the time this can be calculated by eye, but tools are available to help you to measure a precise ¼-inch seam allowance. On a straight-edged template, this can be done by using a perspex ¼-inch ruler (also called a quilter's quarter ruler), available from quilting stores. For a curved template, use a seam tracer. This is a small metal disc with a hole in the center and a groove around the outside. You put a pencil in the hole and the edge of the disk against the edge of the template and roll the seam tracer around the edge of the template to give a precise ¼-inch seam line. Another type of seam tracer consists of two connected pencils with their points ¼ inch apart; one is held against the edge of the template and the other is used to trace around it.

FUSSY-CUTTING

Sometimes you may wish to center or make a feature of a motif. This is known as "fussy-cutting." Use a commercial template with a cut-out center, or make your own from template plastic, as shown in the photograph below. Be sure to include the seam allowance.

Mask off the seam allowance using masking tape to give yourself an accurate "window" to look through. Place the template over the motif and move it around until you are happy with what you see. Trace lightly around the template with a pencil, then cut out the shape.

To make the motif appear in the same place in each fussy-cut piece, mark the edges of the template to show where they overlap with particular elements in the design, and then line up these marks with the relevant parts of the pattern on the fabric each time you cut a new piece.

CREATING HEXAGONS

Hexagons are easily made from sets of six 60-degree triangles. (These add up to 360 degrees, making a full circle in the center.)

First create a half-hexagon by sewing together three 60-degree triangles. Create another half-hexagon in the same way.

The hexagon can be joined in one of two ways. The first is simply to sew the two halves across the middle, taking care to match the points in the center. This method is used in Brighton Rock (page 12). In the other method, the half-hexagons are joined to other shapes (for example, triangles or diamonds) in horizontal rows. When these rows are joined, whole hexagons are formed. This is the method used in Jazz Hands (page 168) and Erica's Honesty (page 176), below left.

Diagram 5
Forming a hexagon from
60-degree triangles

Left: Jazz Hands (page 168) and Erica's Honesty (page 176) are both created using hexagons.

HAND-PIECING

Sometimes—such as when sewing small hexagons or other pieces with set-in seams—hand-piecing is easier than machine-piecing. When hand-piecing, the fabric pieces are put together with the right sides facing and the seam lines (rather than the raw edges) even. Use a short, fine needle and a matching sewing thread. Begin sewing with a small backstitch, then sew along the seam line using a small running stitch. Every five or six stitches, take another backstitch for strength. End with another small backstitch, then fasten off.

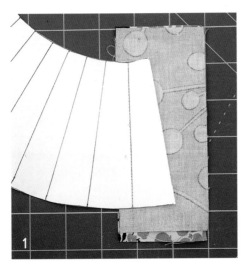

FOUNDATION-PIECING

Foundation-piecing is a thrifty technique, used to make blocks of exactly the same size, to achieve accurate designs with sharp points or to stabilize scraps and control bias stretching.

It involves, as the name implies, the use of paper or fabric as a base, or foundation, for piecing. Lines drawn on the underside of the foundation enable straight accurate seams that allow even the most advanced blocks to be sewn perfectly. Fabric used to stabilize strips adds an extra layer of support, as well as warmth, if needed.

In this book, Gypsy Kisses (page 132) and Fruit Tingles (page 140) use the paper method for accurate seams, working with bias as well as points. Foundation papers can be purchased in quilt or craft shops. The block designs need to be traced or copied onto the papers, so you will need at least one page per block. There are several good brands of foundation papers available, and when you're looking, be sure to find one that feeds into your printer or photocopier. In some cases, it is possible to use standard copier paper. However, if seams intersect, this is not a good option. The paper gets removed once the blocks are sewn, and this task can be extremely tedious if the paper cannot be removed easily.

The first step when using the paper method is to trace or copy the pattern for the desired number of blocks onto the foundation paper. Set your sewing machine to a small stitch, say 1.5, which helps when the time comes to remove the papers. Sewing through the paper will dull your needle, so remember to change to a fresh needle when doing other sewing.

Counter-clockwise, from left: 1. Position the foundation paper on top of the two fabric strips and stitch along the marked line. 2. Trim the seam allowance back to $1/4$ inch. 3. Proceed in this way along the foundation shape. 4. Flip the strips to the right side and finger-press before adding each next strip.

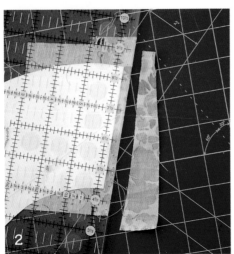

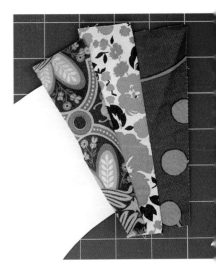

The only tricky part about foundation paper piecing is that you work from the back of the paper when sewing along the seam lines. The fabrics need to be placed right sides together with the wrong side against the paper. Hold the paper up to a light to be sure that the fabric covers the necessary space. Be aware of where the fabric will be sewn and be sure that it covers the next seam line when pressed flat. Sew the line, trim off the excess seam allowance, then flip the strip and press in place. Be sure to leave a ¼-inch seam allowance on the last strip.

When the block is completely stitched, fold over the first strip at the seam and finger-press along the sewing line. Use a seam ripper to gently help loosen the paper. Do not rip out the paper or the stitches will loosen.

In this book, Pop Stars (page 118) and Maple Leaf Rag (124) use muslin as a permanent stabilizer for the blocks. Any lightweight fabric can be used for this process, but be sure that the fabric does not have strong designs that will show through the top fabrics. With a fabric foundation, you don't mark the sewing lines onto the fabric. Simply pin the strip in place, sew through all three layers on the right side, flip the sewn strip into place, press, and continue until the point.

When using either method, it is handy to set up the ironing board next to the sewing machine, as a nice press makes this a very accurate method of sewing. It is a good technique for crazy-piecing, as any size scrap can be used to fill the fabric foundation. It is also good for blocks like log cabin, which need precision sewing.

MACHINE-PIECING TECHNIQUES

Piecing by machine requires accurate and precise seams. The standard seam allowance is ¼ inch. If you plan to do a lot of machine-piecing, a ¼-inch sewing-machine foot will be a good investment.

Machine-piecing is, by its very nature, much faster than hand-piecing, but by employing a technique called chain-piecing, you can make it faster still. To chain-piece, do not lift the presser foot and cut the thread each time you finish a seam. Instead, once you finish the seam on one unit (such as a pair of triangles, as shown below), sew a little beyond the end of the seam. The reel and bobbin threads will entwine to make a "chain." Put another unit under the presser foot and repeat the process until you have sewn all the units. Cut the chains between each unit and press the units open, pressing the seam toward the darker piece. Join the units to other components. Many parts of a quilt can be chain-pieced in this manner, saving both time and thread.

Below: Beginning to chain-piece two half-square triangles. **Center:** Once the seam on the first pair is complete, the next pair is fed into the machine without snipping the thread. **Right:** Continue in this manner to create strings of pairs. When all the pairs are stitched, the "chained" threads between the pairs are cut and the completed units pressed open.

Above: Your appliqué stitches should just catch the finger-pressed edge of the fabric and be quite small and close together.

APPLIQUÉ

There are various appliqué techniques; those used in this book are the iron-on method (page 200), used in Calling It Curtains (page 44), and the needle-turn method (below), used in The Seasons (page 28), Now & Then (page 68), Charlotte Sometimes (page 74), Gypsy Kisses (page 132), Fruit Tingles (page 140), Bluebirds & Happiness (page 150), and Looking Back (page 158), which also features reverse appliqué (page 200). Whatever appliqué method you choose, complete all the appliqué before piecing the blocks together, unless otherwise instructed.

Before beginning the appliqué, decide where you want your shapes to sit on the background block. Use a sharp 2B pencil or other marker to lightly trace the shapes onto the background fabric. A light box is useful when tracing; if you don't have one, an alternative is to lightly tape the design to be traced onto a sunny window, position and tape the fabric over it, and then trace the design.

Remember that some designs will need to have their various elements sewn down in a particular order. For example, when sewing a flower, the stem will need to be sewn first so that it sits under the flower petals, and then the petals added, and lastly the flower center and the leaves. If you are working a complicated appliqué design and you think you might get confused, draw or photocopy a diagram of the complete design, determine the order in which the pieces need to be laid down, and then number the shapes on the diagram so you can keep track.

SARAH'S NEEDLE-TURN APPLIQUÉ

These instructions are for my method of appliqué, which is quite different to a lot of traditional methods. I find it to be both an easy method to use and also an easy method for beginners, as it requires much less preparation than many traditional methods.

The first step is to trace the template shapes onto template plastic or cardboard using a very sharp 2B pencil. Using paper scissors (not your fabric scissors), cut out along the line.

Place the template down on the front of the fabric and trace around it. I use a silver gel pen for marking my sewing lines. I like to use a gel pen for several reasons, but the first and foremost thing you need to know about a gel pen is that it does not wash off. Once you have traced your shape onto the fabric, you're married to it, so be careful with that tracing!

The reasons for the gel pen are, firstly, that it's reflective. I only use silver, not anything else, because the silver shows up on fabric of any color, and the bonus is that it reflects in the light, making it easy to see, day or night. Secondly, it also makes it really easy to see whether you have turned your shape under neatly or not. If you can still see silver, you haven't got the shape right!

Trace the shape or shapes you are going to appliqué onto the right side of the fabric with the gel pen. Take care to leave space between the pieces for a seam allowance. Cut the shapes out a scant ¼ inch from the gel line. Finger-press along the line all around the shape, including into any curves or points. Do not be tempted to iron the press in—a finger-pressed line is easy to manipulate, whereas an ironed line is difficult to change if you iron a point into a crease or a line in the wrong spot. You will also be very likely to burn your fingers!

Position the pieces on the background block using the lightly traced outline or the photograph supplied with the pattern as a guide. Take into account which parts of the various pieces may go under others; dotted lines on the template pieces indicate which parts of each piece should be placed under the adjacent pieces.

Instead of pins, I use appliqué glue to fix the pieces to be sewn onto the background. This is my all-time favorite appliqué gadget! You can glue all the appliqué shapes onto a quilt and then carry all the bits around with you, never having to worry that the pins have come out, or that anything is going to poke you in your sewing bag! You only need a little bit, just a few dots on each shape to make them stick. Leave a few minutes for the glue to dry. Remember that if the glue smudges it doesn't matter, as it is easily able to be peeled back later or washed off.

Thread your appliqué needle with thread to match the appliqué fabric. You should always match your appliqué thread to the shape that you are appliquéing, not to the background. I use very long, fine straw needles for appliqué: the finer the needle, the smaller you can make your stitches for invisible appliqué. You can start anywhere, but try never to start on an inside curve, if you can avoid it.

Tie a knot in the thread and come up from the back to the front of the quilt, catching the very edge of the fabric with your needle. Go down into the background fabric right next to where you came up, run your needle along underneath the back, and come up again right on the edge of the shape. Don't try to turn the whole edge under before you sew it; just turn under the small section you are working on. This makes it easier to keep track of that gel pen and make sure that you turn it all under.

Sew all around the cut edge in this manner. Your stitches should just catch the edge of the fabric and be quite small and close together, which will make the appliqué strong and avoid its being torn or looking puckered.

When you get to a point, the best way to get a nice sharp point is this: sew all the way up to the point on one side. Fold the fabric down 90 degrees under the point, and then sweep the remaining fabric downward and underneath the main part of the point. Take a stitch right at the point again and give it a sharp tug. In the words of my favorite appliqué teacher, Becky Goldsmith from Piece O Cake Designs, this just "makes it feel pointier"! Continue sewing down the other side of the point.

IRON-ON METHOD

This method requires double-sided fusible webbing. This has a paper-side, which is smooth, and a glue-side, which is rough. Trace the desired shape onto the paper-side and cut out roughly, using paper scissors. Using a hot iron, press the roughly cut shapes onto the back of the fabrics with the glue side down. It is vital that the glue side is down, or the shape will stick to your iron.

Using sharp fabric scissors, cut the shapes out of the fabric along the pencil line. Peel the paper off the fabric, leaving the webbing stuck to the back of the fabric. Turn the shapes right side up and position them onto your background fabric. Now iron the pieces down so that they stick to the background panel.

Hand- or machine-appliqué around the edges of the shapes. If you are appliquéing by machine, set your blanket stitch to a width of 1.5 and a length of 2.

Try the stitch out on scrap fabric to ensure you are happy with the result, then stitch around the shapes as above.

When you get to an inside curve, you've reached your next challenge! You can sew all around the outside curves without clipping, but an inside curve needs clipping. Using very sharp, small scissors, carefully clip into the silver line, about ¼ inch apart, all around the inner curve.

I never clip anything until I am ready to sew it. If you do, it just leaves the way open for things to fray and get messy. Sew all the way up to the curve before you clip, and then sew the curve right away.

Continue until you have sewn all around the outside of the shape, and tie the thread off at the back with a small knot.

Turn the block over and make a small cut at the back of the shape, taking care not to cut the appliqué. Cut the background away underneath the appliqué. Be sure not to cut closer than ¼ inch away from the seam lines. Although it is not strictly necessary, removing the fabric in this way makes the appliqué sit nicely and creates fewer layers to quilt through, especially where appliqué pieces overlap.

Repeat this process with each shape in turn. Remove the background from under each piece before applying the next one.

REVERSE APPLIQUÉ

Instead of adding a design on top of a background fabric, in reverse appliqué, a shape in the top fabric is cut away to reveal the background fabric beneath. Reverse appliqué helps to create a different depth in your sewing by taking the eye into the shape you are appliquéing instead of adding to the top of it.

Using the gel pen, trace the shape you are reversing onto the top fabric. Baste the fabric to be revealed behind the top fabric, using appliqué glue, approximately ¼ inch to the outside of the gel pen line. Leave to dry for a few seconds.

Using your thumb and forefinger, pinch the top fabric in the outlined shape away from the underneath fabric so you have two separate pieces. While they are held apart, clip a small hole in the top fabric, using very sharp small scissors. Carefully clip the top fabric away, leaving a scant ¼-inch seam allowance inside the gel pen line. Finger-press around the gel line. Clip any inside curves, and then sweep the fabric underneath the top fabric and stitch in place, revealing the underneath fabric below as you go.

If the shape you are sewing has another layer of reverse appliqué, repeat the technique by basting, cutting, and sewing.

Below: For reverse appliqué, carefully clip away the top fabric with very sharp scissors, leaving a scant ¼-inch seam allowance.

Below: Sweep the seam allowance under as you stitch the edge of the top fabric in place, revealing the underneath fabric.

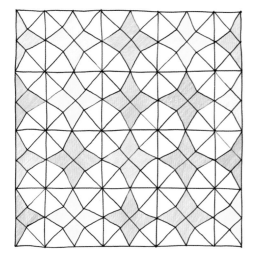

Above: A Quilt Assembly Diagram shows in stylized form how all the blocks of a quilt fit together.
Below: A design wall is invaluable for allowing you to test color choices as well as move finished blocks around until you are happy with their placement.

QUILT LAYOUT

The Quilt Assembly Diagram provided in the pattern will show you how the various components are assembled. There are numerous ways of laying out a quilt. In a square-set quilt, the blocks, sashing strips, and borders are set parallel with the sides and top of the quilt. When a quilt is set "on point," the blocks are at a 45-degree angle to the top and sides of the quilt. This method requires the addition of triangles (known as setting triangles) at the corners and along the sides of the rows to square up the quilt.

Always refer to the assembly diagram for the quilt you are making, rather than relying on a photograph. Many quilt designs, especially complex ones using more than one type of block, feature optical illusions caused by the way in which the various components are combined. Sometimes the logic of the quilt's construction will not become clear until you look at the assembly or layout diagram.

USING A DESIGN WALL

If you're making a scrappy quilt or one that has a lot of blocks of different colors or tones, it's a good idea to lay them all out on a flat surface, such as the floor or a wall, or a design wall, made with batting or felt, which helps

the cut shapes to stay in place. By doing this, it is possible to "audition" or sample colors or shapes before committing to sewing them together. You can move the blocks about until you get a pleasing arrangement. Check that the same fabrics aren't too close to each other and that the eye is not drawn to particular blocks or areas at the expense of the rest of the design. Squinting at the quilt or looking at it through the lens of a camera can help you discern "holes" or unbalanced areas. It is always a good idea to lay out the blocks and step back. However, if this isn't possible, cover a piece of cardboard with batting scraps and keep it next to the sewing machine. Lay out each block on the batting before sewing it together.

ADDING BORDERS

Borders may be added for decorative effect, or to increase the quilt's size, or both. They may have squared-off or mitered corners. The quilt pattern will tell you what length to cut the borders, but you should always measure your quilt before cutting the border fabric, then adjust the length of the border strips if necessary.

Measure in both directions through the middle of the quilt rather than along the edges. This is because the edges may have distorted a little during the making of the quilt, especially if any of the edge pieces are bias cut. Use these measurements to calculate the length of each border, remembering to add seam allowance.

If adding squared-off borders, the side borders will be the length of the quilt top, plus seam allowance. The top and bottom borders will be the width of the quilt top with the side borders added, plus seam allowance. Unless a pattern indicates otherwise, sew the side borders on first, press the seams toward the border, and then add the top and bottom borders.

If adding borders with mitered corners, each border will need to be the width or length of the quilt, plus twice the width of the border to allow enough fabric for mitering, plus seam allowance. Sew each border to the edge of the quilt, beginning and ending the seam a precise ¼ inch from the edge of the quilt. Fold the quilt so that the side and the top are flush, and the two border strips extend out to the side. Use your ruler and a 45-degree-angle line to mark a line from the ¼-inch point to the edge of the strip. Sew along this line and check before cutting to be sure it lies flat. When confident, trim off the extra fabric, and repeat for all four corners.

TYPES OF BATTING

Some battings need to be quilted closer together than others to stop them from drifting around within the quilt or fragmenting when washed.

Polyester batting requires less quilting than cotton or wool batting. However, some polyester battings have a tendency to "fight" the sewing machine.

Wool battings (usually actually a wool/polyester or a wool/cotton blend) provide more warmth and comfort than polyester battings. However, they require more quilting, and those that are not needle-punched tend to pill. Needle-punched wool blends are more stable and require less quilting.

Traditional cotton battings require a lot of quilting, as much as every $1/2$–3 inches. Needle-punched cotton battings are more stable and can be quilted up to about 10 inches apart.

QUILT ASSEMBLY

LAYERING THE QUILT

Once you have added all the borders, and before you can begin quilting, you need to assemble or "sandwich" all three layers of the quilt.

The batting and backing should both be about 4 inches larger all around than the quilt top. You may need to join two widths of fabric, or add a strip of scraps or leftover blocks, to obtain a large enough piece for the backing. We tell you to buy so many yards of backing fabric, just so you know, but if you can piece your backing from fabrics that you already have, then go right ahead. It's the back of the quilt, but you can still be creative!

Press the quilt top and backing. Lay the backing right side down on a large, flat, clean surface (preferably one that is not carpeted), smooth it out carefully, and then tape it to the surface using masking tape. Tape it at intervals along all sides, but do not tape the corners, as this will cause the bias to stretch out of shape.

Place the batting on top of the backing and smooth it out. If you need to join two pieces of batting to get the right size, abutt them and machine-zigzag a seam.

On top of the batting, place the well-pressed quilt top, right side up, ensuring that the top and backing are square to each other. Smooth it out. The three layers must now be basted together to be ready for quilting.

Left: The pressed backing fabric is laid face down on the floor, smoothed out carefully, and taped down.

Center: The batting is placed smoothly on top of the backing.

Right: The pressed quilt top is placed face-up on top of the batting.

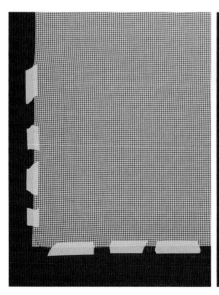

BASTING

Basting can be done with safety pins or long hand-stitches.

If using safety pins, start from the center of the quilt and pin through all three layers at intervals of about 8 inches. If you are intending to machine-quilt, make sure the pins are kept away from the lines to be quilted. Once the whole quilt is safety-pinned in this manner, it can be moved. Safety pins can be used for hand-quilting, but be mindful that they can get in the way of your hoop.

If you are intending to hand-quilt, baste the whole quilt both horizontally and vertically, from the center out, using long hand-stitches at intervals of about 6 inches. Using a curved needle is a good idea, as this makes the task easier on the wrists.

Do not baste using hand-stitches if you intend to machine-quilt, as the basting threads will get caught under the presser foot.

Some quilting stores offer a machine-basting service. This can be a worthwhile investment, especially if you are going to be doing fine hand-quilting in the traditional manner, a task that can take months or even years.

Remove the basting stitches or safety pins only once all the quilting has been completed.

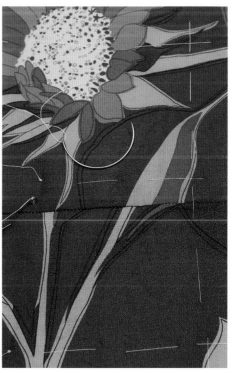

Top right: A quilt that has been commercially machine-basted using long stitches. **Above:** Basting using safety pins. **Right:** Hand-basting using a curved needle.

MACHINE-QUILTING

You may want to machine-quilt your quilt yourself, but we use and recommend a professional quilting service, for a couple of good reasons.

Firstly, finished quilts are usually quite large and, consequently, rather cumbersome. It really is a fairly tricky job to manipulate the bulk of the quilt on a domestic sewing machine, even using a specialized "walking foot." Having pieced your precious quilt so carefully, it would be a shame to spoil it now with puckers and distortions.

Secondly, professional machine-quilters offer a large range of quilting patterns to suit every need and taste and can also advise you on a design that will enhance all your careful work.

QUILTING

Quilting can be fairly rudimentary, its main purpose being to hold together the layers of the quilt, or it can be decorative and sometimes extremely elaborate. Machine-quilting is quick, but nothing beats hand-quilting for sheer heirloom beauty.

Designs for hand-quilting, or elaborate designs for machine-quilting, are generally marked on the quilt top before the quilt's layers are sandwiched together. On pale fabrics, the marking is done lightly in pencil; on dark fabrics, use a special quilter's silver pencil. Pencil lines can be erased later.

If you intend to quilt straight lines or a cross-hatched design, masking tape can be used to mark out the lines on the quilt top. Such tape comes in various widths, from ¼ inch upwards. Free-flowing lines can be drawn on with a chalk pencil.

If you intend to outline-quilt by machine, you may be able to sew straight enough lines by eye; if not, you will need to mark the quilt top first.

HAND-QUILTING

Quilting by hand produces a softer line than machine-quilting, and will give an heirloom quality to quilts. Most of the quilts in this book are quilted using perle cotton, since it is often easier for beginners to work with than finer thread and stands out vividly against the fabric's surface, although traditional quilting thread can be used if you prefer.

To quilt by hand, the fabric needs to be held in a frame (also known as a quilting hoop). Free-standing frames are available, but hand-held ones are cheaper, more portable, and just as effective. One edge of a hand-held

The hand-quilting action, from left:

1. Insert the needle through all three layers.

2. Without pushing the needle through, rock the needle back to the top of the quilt and use your underneath finger to push the tip of the needle up.

3. Push the needle through the fabric to make one stitch.

4. To take several stitches at once, push the needle along the required stitch length, and then dip into the fabric again.

5. Gently pull the stitches to indent the stitch line, always working toward yourself.

frame can be leaned against a table or bench to enable you to keep both your hands free.

Hand-quilting, like machine-quilting, should commence in the center of the quilt and proceed outward. To commence hand-quilting, place the plain (inner) ring of the frame under the center of the quilt. Position the other ring, with the screw, over the top of the quilt to align with the inner ring. Tighten the screw so that the fabric in the frame becomes firm, but not drum-tight.

For traditional quilting, choose the smallest needle that you feel comfortable with. For perle quilting, use a good quality crewel embroidery needle. Thread the needle with about 18 inches of thread. Knot the end of the thread and take the needle down through the quilt top into the batting, a short distance from where you want to start quilting. Tug the thread slightly so that the knot pulls through into the batting, making the starting point invisible. Proceed as follows:

The hand-quilting action

With your dominant hand above the quilt and the other beneath, insert the needle through all three layers at a time, with the middle or index finger of your dominant hand (use a metal thimble to make this easier), until you can feel the tip of the needle resting on your finger at the back. Without pushing the needle through, rock the needle back to the top of the quilt and use your underneath finger to push the tip of the needle up. Put your upper thumb down in front of the needle tip while pushing up from the back. This will make a small "hill" in the fabric. Push the needle through the fabric. This makes one stitch. To take several stitches at once, push the

FASTENING OFF A THREAD

Hold the thread out to the side with your left hand, and loop a one-loop knot using the needle. Slide the loose knot down the thread until it lies directly on the quilt top, and tighten the knot. Take the needle back down through the hole the thread is coming out of and slide it away through the batting. Bring the needle back up to the top of the quilt and give the thread a tug.

The knot will follow down into the hole and lodge in the batting. Cut the thread close to the surface.

needle along to the required stitch length, dip the tip into the fabric, and repeat the above technique. Gently pull the stitches to indent the stitch line evenly. You should always quilt toward yourself, as this reduces hand and shoulder strain, so turn the quilt in the required direction. You can protect your underneath finger using a stick-on plastic shield, such as a Thimble-It. You can also use a leather thimble: however, this does make it more difficult to feel how far the needle has come through, and thus more difficult to keep your stitches even.

To move a short distance from one part of the quilting design to another, push the tip of the needle through the batting and up at the new starting point. Take care not to drag a dark thread under a light fabric, as the line will show.

When you come to the edge of the hoop, leave the thread dangling so that you can pick it up and continue working with it once you have repositioned the hoop. Work all the quilting design within the hoop before repositioning the hoop and beginning to quilt another area. If you need to quilt right up to the border edge, baste lengths of spare cotton fabric to the edge of the quilt, thus giving you enough fabric area to position the edges of the quilt under the quilting hoop.

To fasten off a length of thread, see instructions at left.

Below: Graphic fabric designs offer interesting quilting opportunities, such as this beautiful border fabric used in Erica's Honesty (page 176), which just begged to be outline-quilted.

BINDING

From the width of the binding fabric, cut enough strips of fabric to equal the outside edge of your quilt, plus about 6 inches, to allow for mitered corners and for the ends to be folded under. Binding fabrics are usually (though not always) cut into strips 2½ inches wide; follow the instructions in the pattern.

Seam the strips into a continuous length, making the joins at 45-degree angles, as shown to the left. To do this, fold under one end at a 45-degree angle and finger-press a crease. Unfold. The crease line will become the seam line. Mark this line lightly with a pencil. With right sides together and the two fabric pieces at 90 degrees, align the angled cut end with another strip of binding fabric. Align the ¼-inch measurement on a quilter's ruler with this line and trim off the corner. Sew the two strips together along the marked line. Press all seams to one side and trim off the "ears."

Press the entire strip in half along its length. Doubling the fabric like this makes the binding more durable.

Trim the backing and the batting so that they are even with the edge of the quilt top. Beginning at one end of the binding strip, pin the binding to one edge of the quilt, starting about 4 inches in from a corner and having the raw edges even. Machine-sew in place through all the layers of the quilt, using a ¼-inch seam allowance and mitering the corners. To miter corners, end the seam ¼ inch from the corner and fasten off. Fold the binding fabric up at a 45-degree angle, and then fold it down so that the fold is level with the edge of the binding just sewn. Begin the next seam at the edge of the quilt and proceed as before. Repeat this process to miter all the corners.

When you approach the point at which the binding started, trim the excess, neatly tuck the end of the binding under itself, and stitch the rest of the seam.

Press the binding away from the quilt. Turn the binding to the back of the quilt and slipstitch the folded edge in place by hand to finish. Your quilt is now complete!

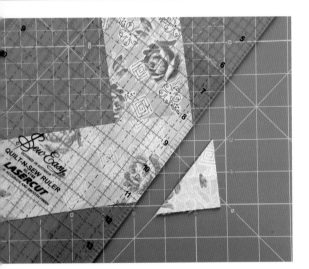

Top: Detail of the backing and binding of Gypsy Kisses (page 132).

Center: Preparing to join two lengths of binding fabric at a 45-degree angle.

Below: The finished join, ready to be pressed to one side.

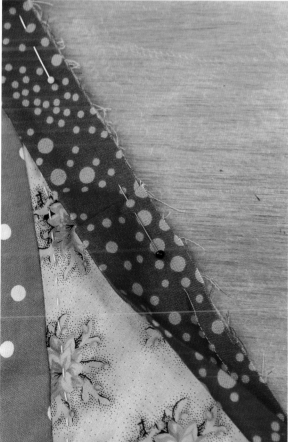

Above: Machine-sewing the binding to the front of the quilt.

Left: When you approach the point at which the binding begins, fold the end under to make a neat finish.

Below: Slipstitch the binding neatly to the back of the quilt.

Glossary & Index

Glossary

APPLIQUÉ A technique in which small pieces of fabric are attached to a background fabric. They may be stitched on by hand or by machine, or ironed on using fusible webbing.

BACKING The undermost layer of a quilt.

BASTING A method of holding together several layers of fabric during quilting, so that they do not move around. Basting may be done using a long hand-stitch, or with safety pins. The stitches or pins are removed once the quilting is complete.

BATTING The middle layer of a quilt; also known as wadding.

BIAS The diagonal of a woven fabric, at a 45-degree angle to the straight grain (the warp and weft). Fabric cut on the bias stretches, so care must be taken when handling and sewing bias-cut pieces.

BINDING The narrow strips of fabric (usually made of a double thickness) that enclose the raw edges and batting of a quilt.

BLOCK The basic unit of a quilt top. Blocks are usually square, but may be rectangular, hexagonal, or other shapes. They may be plain (of one fabric only), appliquéd, or pieced.

BORDER A strip of fabric (plain, appliquéd, or pieced) joined to the central panel of a quilt and used to frame it and also to add extra size.

CHAIN-PIECING A method of joining fabric pieces by machine in an assembly-line fashion, which speeds up the process and uses less thread. Pairs or sets of block pieces are fed into the machine, one after the other, without snipping the threads between them.

CROSS-HATCHING A quilting pattern of parallel, equidistant lines that run in two directions to form a grid of squares or diamonds.

DITCH-STITCHING Quilting along a seam line. It should be done on the low side of the seam, through three layers, not five; also called stitching in the ditch.

EASE To make two pieces of fabric of different size fit together in one seam. One piece may have to be stretched or gathered slightly to bring it to the required length. To ease, first pin the pieces at intervals until they fit, then sew them.

ECHO-QUILT To quilt around the shape of a piece, inside or outside the seam, matching its outline.

FAT QUARTER A piece of fabric that is made by cutting a yard of fabric in halves, first vertically, then horizontally. The piece thus cut is approximately 18 x 22 inches (or 50 x 56 cm in metric measurements).

FEED DOGS The teeth under the sewing plate of a sewing machine, which move to pull the fabric through the machine. The feed dogs must be lowered to allow for free-motion quilting.

FINGER-PRESSING A way of pressing a temporary crease in a piece of fabric, for example, when finding the middle of two pieces so that they can be matched before being joined. Running a fingernail along a crease will make it lie flat.

FOUR-PATCH A block with two, four, or multiples of four units per block.

FUSIBLE WEBBING A fabric that has been coated with an adhesive that fuses fabric pieces together when pressed with a warm iron. May be fusible on only one side (fusible interfacing) or both (appliqué webbing). Fusible webbing is used to stabilize fine fabrics or to attach appliqué pieces to background fabric.

FUSSY-CUTTING A method of selectively cutting a piece of fabric so as to showcase a particular motif, such as a large flower. Fussy cutting is most easily done using a see-through template that allows you to position the motif to its best advantage within the template area.

GRAIN The direction of the fabric, along the warp (vertical threads) or the weft (horizontal threads). These are both straight grains, along which woven fabrics do not stretch. Compare with Bias.

HALF-SQUARE TRIANGLE A triangle made from a square cut across one diagonal. Half-square triangles have the bias along the hypotenuse. Compare with Quarter-square Triangle.

LOFT A term referring to the thickness of batting (wadding). A high-loft batting is thicker and fluffier than a low-loft batting.

MITERED CORNER A corner that is joined at a 45-degree angle.

MOTIF A design element or image used in a printed fabric, quilt block, or appliqué block, for example, a heart motif or floral motif.

MUSLIN A plain, usually undyed, cotton fabric that may be bleached or unbleached. A fine-weave muslin, known as quilter's muslin, is often used as the background for appliqué or quilt blocks.

ON POINT An arrangement in which the quilt blocks are placed diamond-fashion, with their corners at the 12, 3, 6, and 9 o'clock positions, rather than in a square fashion.

ONE-PATCH Any quilt design that uses a single-shaped piece, such as a hexagon, square, or triangle, for the pieced top.

OUTLINE-QUILT To make one or more outlines of a motif or block design, radiating outwards.

PATCH *See* Piece.

PATCHWORK A generic term for the process of sewing together many small pieces of fabric to make a quilt. Also known as piecework.

PIECE An individual fabric shape that may be joined to other fabric shapes to make a quilt block, or used on its own (in which case it is known as a one-patch). Also known as a patch.

PIECING The process of joining together pieces of fabric to make a quilt top, a quilt block, or a border.

PIN-BASTE To pin through the layers of a quilt "sandwich," using safety pins to hold them together during quilting. The pins are removed once the quilting is complete.

QUARTER-SQUARE TRIANGLE A triangle that is made from a square cut across both diagonals. Quarter-square triangles have the bias along the two short sides.

QUILT TOP The uppermost, decorative layer of a quilt. It may be pieced, appliquéd, or a combination of both, with or without borders.

QUILTER'S RULERS Precision-cut, straight-edged plastic rulers in various sizes, used with rotary cutters and rotary-cutting mats. They make it easy to cut accurate shapes, and to cut through several layers of fabric at once. They come in straight varieties and also those designed for cutting at various angles or for creating triangles.

QUILTING Generally speaking, the process of making a quilt; more specifically, the process of stitching patterns by hand or machine into the quilt layers to decorate the quilt, add strength, and anchor the batting inside the quilt.

QUILTING FRAME A free-standing floor apparatus, made of wood or plastic tubing, in which a quilt is held while it is being quilted.

QUILTING HOOP A hand-held circular device in which a quilt is held while being quilted.

RAW EDGE The cut edge of a fabric.

ROTARY CUTTER A cutting device, similar in appearance to a pizza cutter, with a razor-sharp circular blade. Used in conjunction with a quilter's ruler, it allows several layers of fabric to be cut at once easily and with great accuracy.

ROTARY-CUTTING MAT A self-healing plastic mat on which rotary cutters are used, to protect both the blade of the cutter and the work surface beneath the mat.

SASHING Strips of fabric that separate blocks in a quilt, to frame them and/or make the quilt larger.

SEAM ALLOWANCE The margin of fabric between the cut edge and the seam line. For quilting and most appliqué, it is ¼ inch.

SEAM LINE The guideline that is followed while sewing.

SELVAGES The woven finished edges along the length of the fabric.

SETTING The way in which blocks are arranged in a quilt top, for example, square or on point.

SETTING SQUARE A plain block or square used with pieced or appliquéd blocks in a quilt top.

SETTING TRIANGLE A triangle placed between blocks along the side of a quilt set on point, to straighten up the edges.

STASH A quilter's hoard of fabrics.

TEMPLATE PLASTIC Cardboard or paper shapes used for tracing and cutting fabric pieces for piecing or appliqué, or to transfer quilting designs to a quilt top.

WALKING FOOT Sewing-machine foot that feeds the top layer of a quilt sandwich evenly through the machine, while the feed dogs control the bottom layer.

WARP The lengthwise threads in a woven fabric, which interlock with the weft threads. *See also* Weft.

WEFT The widthwise threads in a woven fabric, which interlock with the warp threads. *See also* Warp.

Index

60-degree rulers 192

A
antique quilts 9, 68, 92
appliqué 198–201, 214
  iron-on method 200
  reverse 200
  Sarah's needle-turn method 198
appliqué glue 199

B
backing 204, 214
basting 205, 214
batting 204, 214
bias 214
binding 210–211, 214
block 214
Bluebirds & Happiness 150
borders 203, 214
Brighton Rock 12

C
Calling It Curtains 44
chain-piecing 197, 214
Charlotte Sometimes 74
color 188–189
color wheel 188, 189
Coming Up Roses 108
contrast 188
cross-hatching 214
curved shapes 194
cutting fabric 190
  60-degree cutting 192
  by hand 194
  fussy-cutting 195, 214

D
diamonds 192, 193
directional print 186
ditch-stitching 214

E
ease 214
echo-quilt 214
Erica's Honesty 176

F
fabric 186, 188
  preparing 189
fat quarters 214
feed dogs 214
finger-pressing 214
foundation-piecing 196
four-patch 214
frame 206
Fruit Tingles 140
fusible interfacing/webbing 200, 214
fussy-cutting 195, 214

G
grain 186, 214
graphics 189
Gypsy Kisses 132

H
half-square triangles 190, 191, 214
hand-piecing 196
hand-quilting 206
Heaven & Earth 20
hexagons 195
hoops 206

I
inspiration 8
iron-on appliqué 200

J
Jazz Hands 168
Jungle Boogie 60

K
Kismet 38

L
layering 204
layout 202
  diagram 202
loft 214
Looking Back 158

M
machine-basting service 205
machine-quilting 206
Maple Leaf Rag 124
measurements 186
mitered corners 203, 215
monofilament thread 187
motif 215
muslin 215

N
needle-turn appliqué 198
Now & Then 68

O
on-point layout 202, 215
one-patch 215

outline-quilt 215

Over the Border 84

P

patch 215

patchwork 215

piece 215

piecing 196–197, 215

  foundation- 196

  hand- 196

  machine- 197

pin-baste 215

Playground Days 54

Pop Stars 118

printed fabrics 186

Q

quarter-square triangles 190–192, 215

quilter's quarter ruler 194

quilter's rulers 190–3, 215

quilting (stitching) 206–208, 215

R

raw edge 215

rotary cutter 187, 215

rulers 190–193

  60-degree 192

  half-square 191

  Kaleido-Ruler 190

  quarter-square 191

  specialized 190

  square 190

  standard 190

  wedge 193

S

sashing 215

seam allowance 215

seam line 215

The Seasons 28

selvages 215

setting 202, 215

setting square 215

setting triangle 215

square rulers 190

square-set layout 202

stash 215

Stashbuster 102

Sunday 92

T

template plastic 194

templates 194, 195, 215

threads 187

  fastening off 208

triangles 190–193

W

walking foot 215

warp 215

weft 215

SOURCES FOR SUPPLIES

All fabrics, kits, and accessories
used in the projects in this book
are available from
Material Obsession
144 Pittwater Road
Gladesville NSW 2110
Australia
Phone: +61 (0)2 9817 2733
www.materialobsession.com

Or check your local quilting shop
for materials.

About the Authors

Patchwork and quilting was an unlikely outcome for me. As a child, I had little success with my sewing projects and math was, well … not my favorite subject. However, I always loved art, and found my career heading more and more toward working with color and design. I spent years living in New York City, always watching, digesting influences, and asking questions, all the while wondering what to do with my hands that were itching to make things. My quilting journey started 16 years ago and, in one stitch, became an obsession. It was as if all the influences of my life could now be expressed through patchwork.

I started out slowly, completely self-taught with the aid of library books. Easy patterns and blocks were appealing, so for years the patterns were about squares and rectangles. The simplicity of the square had unending appeal in its diversity as well as simplicity. However, one day I found a 60-degree ruler and suddenly, new possibilities appeared. I found that I could look at something and accurately reproduce it with an acrylic ruler in that shape. From there, drafting blocks, appliqué, and lots of other fun things were only an idea away. The best thing about quilting is that as long as I can see and move my fingers, I can still learn more! Quilting gives my life a thread … a place to call home, a place to be entirely me in an ever-changing world.

There are wonderfully influential people out there doing great things. Kaffe Fassett, Gwen Marsden, Denyse Schmidt, Anna Maria Horner, and others offer gifted inspiration. One look at a palette, a balance of simple lines, or a multi-layered design effect and I am out of control, cutting up bits and sewing them together! It isn't really about the practical act of sewing itself, but rather about the wonder of what can be revealed by that act.

Aside from the quilting passion, I have three gorgeous teenage boys and often find myself listening to discussions about cricket and rugby while preparing food. I love their passion for their sports … games that I did not grow up with and that have a secret language all their own. Quite often, the talk goes right over my head. My husband, John, is a photographer, so our lives have a very visual base. I am lucky to have his vision to help me keep mine in focus. He has a great critical eye for design and is a constant source of analysis. If he doesn't like a quilt, it often ends up as a UFO! We co-exist happily, all doing our own things.

So, really, about this author is probably about the readers as well. The quilting journey can start in an unassuming manner, but soon it swallows us up with endless possibilities and opportunities to share what we do. We see, we make, we enjoy, surrounded by the normal elements of our lives … fabric, family, friends, and food (in any order you choose!). I hope that you enjoy the ideas in this book and stay inspired always.

Kathy Doughty

All my life, I have made things, drawn things, and imagined things. When I was a child, I wanted to own a shop, draw pictures, and write a book… It's not often you can say that your childhood dreams have all come true.

My mother sewed beautifully, always making clothes, embroidering, stitching, and piecing in her sewing room. Her greatest gift to me was her love of making—whether it was with fabric, food, or friendship—and it is a love I hope I can give to my children and my students.

My quilts are like my children—so beautiful to my eyes, possessively treasured, carefully considered, not always perfect, but made with passion! The difference with quilts is that once I am finished with one, I can start right away on another. If that were the way with children, I would be the Old Woman Who Lived in the Shoe!

For me, so much of this book has been about experimentation. These quilts are MORE—more color, more pieces, more techniques, more information, more creativity. In making them, I have expanded myself, worked outside my comfort zone, and spent many hours pondering borders, auditioning fabrics, mixing colors, and drafting, drawing, cutting, pinning, sewing, quilting, and, yes—sometimes unpicking!

I am never happier than when I'm in my sewing room, with the dog asleep under the machine, my two boys doing their homework on the other side of the desk, and my husband lounging in the

doorway with a glass of wine. It is the smallest room in the house (and the most cluttered!) but somehow, it is where we all end up at the close of the day, after school and before dinner.

My life is full of new opportunities because of quilting. New students, new staff, new experiences, new ideas. I hope that my quilts convey some of that sense of discovery to you, and that you can create a similar buzz of happiness from making your own.

Sarah Fielke

Acknowledgments

In the spirit of sharing inspiration, I would like to thank: ✤ The most inspiring people in my life, starting with John for his time and patience in life, as well as for the seemingly endless task of photographing the quilts for this book. Without his eye, I would have so much less vision. ✤ Oscar, Noah, and Sam for sharing their days, while turning into such beautiful young men, and for their occasional opinion. ✤ My lovely mom and fair-minded dad and the rest of the American family that still remembers me! ✤ Gai and Brownyn who drop in to review the design wall. ✤ Cut Loose, Hunters Hill Quilters, and all my quilting friends, who listen and consider choices. ✤ Georgina Bitcon, our editor, for her relentless attention to the details in my patterns, and for helping me to learn a process of self-correction that I didn't have before. ✤ The Material Obsession team, of course, for love, energy, input, help, and support, as well as creative influence. That team starts with Sarah—it's our differences that make our strengths shine and the days so entertaining. ✤ And finally, everyone who shares the inspirational quilting spirit for what it is, be you near or far. – *Kathy*

I would like to thank: ✤ Everyone who shares my quilting day with me, whether it is one day a month, one day a week, or every day. ✤ My students and customers, who make working and teaching at Material Obsession such a pleasurable and happy experience. ✤ My friends, near and far, from the blog, as well as the Dolly Quilters, who have made me look forward to turning my computer on every morning, just to see what they are all up to. ✤ The Material Obsession girls, who help us so endlessly and (relatively!) uncomplainingly, and make the corners of the shop ring with laughter. ✤ Georgina, for her patience and humor through the trials of *MO2*. ✤ Beril, Anita, Carolyn, and Erica, who always have time to listen to my troubles and my triumphs. ✤ My dad, who gives me his sage advice whenever I ask. ✤ Charlie, Oscar, and Damian, whose pride and confidence in me is all I will ever need. ✤ And Kathy ... we are on an amazing journey, my friend, and I hope that through the changes, twists, and turns, we always remember that we love each other, and love each other's quilts. – *Sarah*

We would both like to thank:

✤ The owners of our beautiful photography locations: Suzi and Bill Curtis, for their lovely boat shed; Carl and the late Alysoun Ryves, for their wonderful home in Hunters Hill. ✤ The Murdoch team, for their consistently positive approach to our work. ✤ Kim Bradley, for her machine-quilting. ✤ And all the magnificent Material Obsession girls who make it possible for us to function at a fast pace in an arena of constant inspiration: Carolyn Davis, Sheena Chapman, Kate Barclamb, Bundle (Louise) Caldwell, Erica Spinks, Kate Cox, Grace Widders, and Florence Tynan (who adds class to Mondays with her French accent).